Wrestling with the Reformation in Augsburg, 1530

REACTING TO THE PAST is an award-winning series of immersive role-playing games that actively engage students in their own learning. Students assume the roles of historical characters and practice critical thinking, primary source analysis, and argument, both written and spoken. Reacting games are flexible enough to be used across the curriculum, from first-year general education classes and discussion sections of lecture classes to capstone experiences, intersession courses, and honors programs.

Reacting to the Past was originally developed under the auspices of Barnard College and is sustained by the Reacting Consortium of colleges and universities. The Consortium hosts a regular series of conferences and events to support faculty and administrators.

NOTE TO INSTRUCTORS: Before beginning the game, you must download the game materials, including an instructor's manual containing a detailed schedule of class sessions, role sheets for students, and handouts.

To download these essential resources, visit https://reactingconsortium.org/games, click on the page for this title, then click "Game Materials."

Wrestling with the Reformation in Augsburg, 1530

EMILY FISHER GRAY

BARNARD

The University of North Carolina Press

Chapel Hill

© 2023 Reacting Consortium, Inc.
All rights reserved
Manufactured in the United States of America

Cover art: Konfessionsbild, *Presentation of the Augsburg Confession*, St. Johannis, Schweinfurt. Courtesy Wikimedia Commons.

ISBN 978-1-4696-7630-2 (pbk.: alk. paper)
ISBN 978-1-4696-7631-9 (e-book)

Contents

List of Illustrations / vii

1. INTRODUCTION / 1

Prologue: After the Reichstag / 2

Basic Features of Reacting to the Past / 5

    Game Setup / 5

    Game Play / 6

    Game Requirements / 6

Controversy / 7

Counterfactuals / 8

2. HISTORICAL BACKGROUND / 9

Brief Chronology of the Early Reformation / 9

    Augsburg and the Reformation / 9

    Augsburg in the Sixteenth Century / 10

    Late Medieval Religion / 11

    The Reformation Comes to Augsburg, 1517–1524 / 14

    Reformation Radicalism, 1524–1530 / 18

    The Augsburg Reichstag of 1530 / 22

3. THE GAME / 25

Major Issues for Debate / 25

    Issue 1: "Sola Scriptura": Should Priests Be Allowed to Marry? / 26

    Issue 2: Faith versus Works: Should Augsburg's Citizens Be Punished for Eating Meat on Lenten Fast Days? / 26

    Issue 3: Baptism and Original Sin: What Should Be Done about the Anabaptists? / 27

    Issue 4: Art and Iconoclasm: What Should Be Done about the Paintings, Statues, Stained Glass, and Other Ornate Furnishings in the Churches? / 27

Issue 5: The Sacraments: How Should Augsburg's Churches Celebrate the Eucharist? / 28

Political and Military Alliances / 29

Raising Taxes / 30

A Note on Religious Toleration / 32

Rules and Procedures / 32

The Gentlemen's Drinking Club / 33

Hiring Mercenary Soldiers / 33

Sentencing Criminals and Anabaptists / 33

Standard Game Schedule / 34

Game Session 1 / 34

Game Session 2 / 34

Game Session 3 / 34

Game Session 4 / 34

Game Session 5: Postmortem / 35

4. ROLES AND FACTIONS / 37

Roman Faction / 37

Wittenberg Faction / 38

Swiss Faction / 39

Indeterminates (No Assigned Faction) / 40

5. CORE TEXTS / 43

Main Texts: The Three Confessions / 43

The Augsburg Confession (1530), Selections / 43

The Tetrapolitan Confession (1530), Selections / 48

The Confutatio Pontificia (1530), Selections / 52

Supplementary Texts / 58

Ulrich Zwingli, *Of the Clarity and Certainty of the Word of God* (1522) / 58

Johann Maier von Eck, *Enchiridion of Commonplaces and Articles on the New Teachings* (1525), Selections / 59

Martin Luther, *Against the Heavenly Prophets in the Matter of Images and Sacraments* (1525) / 63

The Schleitheim Confession of Faith (1527) / 64

Martin Luther, *The Small Catechism* (1529), Selections / 67

Ulrich Zwingli, Letter to Vadian concerning the Marburg Colloquy (1529) / 68

Philip Melanchthon, *Apology of the Augsburg Confession* (1530), Selections / 70

Interrogations of Suspected Anabaptists (1528, 1533) / 74

Acknowledgments / 77

Appendix: How to Find and Cite Passages from the Old or New Testament / 79

Glossary / 81

Selected Bibliography of English-Language Sources / 85

Illustrations

MAPS

Holy Roman Empire in 1530 / x

South German / Swiss cities / xi

FIGURES

Augsburg in Winter (*Monatsbilder*) / 4

View of Augsburg, Germany / 11

Death and the Preacher (Totentanz) / 13

Martin Luther as an Augustinian Monk / 15

Conrad Peutinger / 16

Portrait of Ulrich Zwingli / 17

The Sausage Seller / 18

Philip Melanchthon Administers the Sacrament of Baptism / 21

Emperor Charles V / 21

Augsburg Confession / 22

Gulden coin, minted in Augsburg / 31

Wrestling with the Reformation in Augsburg, 1530

Holy Roman Empire in 1530

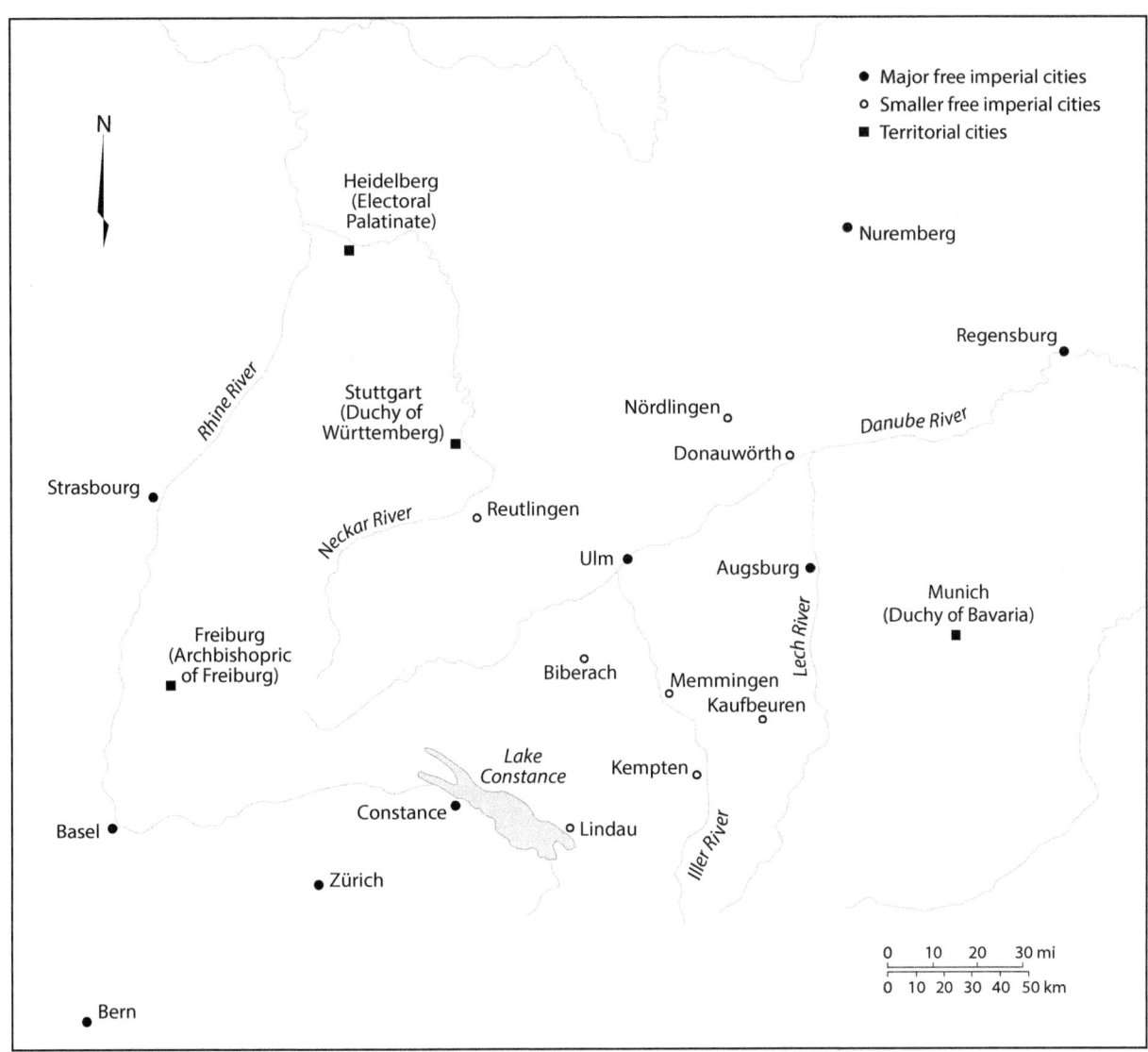

South German / Swiss cities

1 Introduction

In 1517, the obscure Wittenberg **friar** and theologian **Martin Luther** published a critique of the church's practice of selling **indulgences** and touched off a religious revolution. With the support of the Duke of Saxony, Luther doubled down on his demands for church reform and began a movement Rome soon found itself powerless to stop. Other reformers quickly followed Luther, each with a unique vision for reform. Many Swiss and southern German cities gravitated toward the teachings of Zurich priest **Ulrich Zwingli**, who advocated a more thorough reformation than Luther. The radical teachings of **Anabaptist** preachers captured the imaginations of many urban poor and rural peasants. Meanwhile, the church in Rome continued the long process of reforming itself from within while trying to defend against criticism from followers of Luther, Zwingli, and others. But reform came too late to satisfy Rome's critics. The Reformation split Western Christianity into multiple competing sects and forever altered the trajectory of European history.

This Reacting to the Past game transports you to the place where difficult religious, political, social, and economic decisions were made: Augsburg, caught between the peoples' demand for religious reform and the will of a Holy Roman Emperor bent on quashing dangerous dissent. Emperor Charles V chose Augsburg as the site of his Imperial Reichstag in 1530 and brought the princes, bishops, and representatives of the major cities of the empire to Augsburg to discuss resolving the religious conflict. Instead, three distinct and irreconcilable camps emerged, each with its own position statement on the major religious issues. Charles eventually gave up on the notion of religious reconciliation, leaving Augsburg and other principalities within the empire to figure out how to restore communal unity and protect themselves in the new, divided world—where established certainties suddenly came into question, old allies turned against one another, and nothing less than the **salvation** of souls was at stake.

As a member of the city council of Augsburg in 1530, you will have to balance the competing demands of the citizens and the emperor, while considering the implications of various reform positions for the city's military defense, economic growth, and spiritual purity. Should Augsburg adopt the *Augsburg Confession*, a statement of principles presented during the 1530 Reichstag by Martin Luther's Wittenberg colleagues? Or join the **Tetrapolitan** cities that offered an alternate vision of reform influenced by Ulrich Zwingli? Or should Augsburg adopt the *Confutatio Pontificia*, the strong rebuttal to the *Augsburg Confession* written by representatives of the **pope** in Rome and endorsed by the emperor? Decisions about religious practices in Augsburg could provoke a riot from reform-minded citizens or cause Emperor Charles V to make good on his promise to invade the city and revoke its independent charter. Augsburg needs allies, but alliances have suddenly become dependent on the type of reform the city chooses—further complicated by its need to feed the poor, protect its rapid protocapitalist economic growth, and deal with the problem of Anabaptists infiltrating the community.

PROLOGUE: AFTER THE REICHSTAG

The streets of Augsburg are full of hustle and bustle, but they feel comparatively quiet now that the emperor has left. Adding 4,000 people to an already crowded city for six months! I will not miss the Imperial soldiers quartered in my home, taking our beds and leaving us to sleep on the floor. The Bavarian soldiers were loud, boisterous, and demanding, insisting that Augsburg's beer was not nearly as fine as the drink from their own villages. I felt bad for the young Spanish soldier, though, so young and far from home. He was perfectly contented with the beer and always complimented my cooking. Which is more than I can say for my own children, our household servants, and the apprentices who work in my husband's shop. They bolt down their food and fight over any sausages that remain. I almost look forward to **Lent** every year—for forty days, we eat only bread, vegetables, and sometimes fish. It's difficult to follow these restrictions, but nice not worrying about how we can afford expensive meat to fill the bellies of the hungry young people who live in our household.

Prices have stabilized now, with the emperor, princes, bishops—and their hordes of clerks and guards and retainers—finally gone. I may even be able to afford a cut of lamb for supper. My husband will appreciate that. He has worked so hard lately, running our shop during the day and volunteering extra hours helping to run the **guild**. He is young and energetic—he could easily rise to the position of guild master and serve on the city council some day. I can imagine him there, among all the fabulously wealthy merchants and **patricians** in their furs, making decisions that will protect Augsburg and help it continue to grow as a godly community. He may not be rich, and he may not be a member of the exclusive Gentlemen's Drinking Club, but his vote on the council would count as much as theirs.

To give thanks to God for the return of normalcy, I stop in at the Franciscan church on my way to the market. The emperor had ordered this church locked toward the end of the Reichstag in a fruitless attempt to quell the religious disturbances, so I used to have to go all the way across town to Holy Cross to pray. The Franciscan church is as convenient to the radical weavers as it is to me, so it was often full of people whose desire for reform leads them to tear up books and dump salt in the holy water, which the emperor could not abide. I complained to one of my neighbors about the inconvenience, and she unexpectedly invited me to attend an Anabaptist Bible meeting in her home. Tempting as it was to avoid the long walk to a **parish** church, I couldn't quite bring myself to associate with Anabaptists. I hear they refuse to swear oaths and serve in the city guard—and they don't even baptize their infant children!

Luckily, I am almost alone in the Franciscan church today. I nod at the priest working quietly in one corner. He must be as relieved as I am to see things return to normal. It's nice to have a few minutes to pray, enjoying the peace of the church before heading on to the market and the many tasks that await me before sundown. As I kneel before a painting of the Virgin Mary, I remember a sermon I attended a few months ago, during the height of the Reichstag. The preacher, Johannes Schneider, declared that he felt called upon to defy the emperor's restrictions and preach about how the traditional celebration of the **Eucharist** is blasphemy, all prayers should be said in German for the people to understand, and all people should be offered the wine as well as the bread. His words made me feel conflicted. As a small child, I used to gaze in wonder through the wooden screen at the front of the church as the priests murmured in Latin, transforming the morsels of bread and cup of wine on the altar into the body and blood of God. On the rare occasions ordinary people are allowed to take communion, I like the idea of being able to taste the wine and not just the bread. But the words of the priest's German prayer do not have quite the same mystical power as they do in Latin. Despite my ambivalence, the fact that Schneider felt strongly enough about these issues to risk arrest gives me pause. He was, in fact, arrested almost immediately after that sermon, though what happened to him next is a matter of dispute. Some people claim that he was dragged from his cell in the night and drowned in the river, but others insist that he escaped. Either way, it seems an extreme penalty for following his conscience, even though I am not sure whether I agree with his argument. I look into the eyes of the Virgin in the image before me. She stares over my head, offering no answers to my questions.

I sigh and rise from my knees. There are tasks to be done, and the best cuts of meat will be gone from the market if I don't get there soon. The market square is in the center of town, beneath the protective shadow of the Perlach Tower. Mercenary soldiers hired by the city council climb the tower every day to watch for danger; if strong storms approach, or fire breaks out, or they see an invading army coming our way, they will ring the bells so everyone knows it's time for women to take cover and men to spring into action to protect the city. These days, I rather suspect they are watching for signs of internal rather than external dangers. Paid soldiers have manned the tower since an urban insurrection six years ago threatened the council. I wonder if the soldiers see me now, rushing along to the market. I can't help feeling that I would much prefer to have my fellow citizens from the volunteer town guard up there watching, rather than foreigners from who knows where, even if our own council pays their salaries.

I arrive at the market and rush to the butcher's row. I am in luck: my friend is working her stall, selling meat that her husband and his apprentices have procured and cut. She sees me and grins, pulling a lamb haunch from beneath the counter. "I thought you might come today! I set this aside just for you." I don't need to inspect the meat or haggle over the price—I trust her to treat me fairly. She has saved me some juicy gossip as well as meat, so we sit and chat for a while. Another priest has announced his intention to marry. A young day laborer has been arrested for disturbing the peace by throwing rocks over the garden walls of wealthy citizens. A thief and two unlicensed prostitutes are across the market, publicly

Jörg Breu, *Augsburg in Winter (Monatsbilder)*, 1531–50. Deutsches Historisches Museum, Berlin. Wikimedia Commons.

imprisoned in the stocks. Our city rarely puts criminals to death, preferring fines or public humiliation. In some instances, criminals are banished. Only in serious cases are offenders sentenced to death, such as the two weavers who were executed for their roles in the 1524 uprising—though it is an open question whether they were really the ringleaders or simply scapegoats to make the city council appear strong and decisive.

As we talk, I see a small child sneak toward a fruit seller's stall and steal an apple. The old woman running the stall lets out a shriek and begins to give chase, but her aged legs are no match for those of a young and hungry boy. Shoppers and merchants halfheartedly attempt to intercept the child, but he escapes up Maximilian Street, past the imposing facades of the merchant and banking houses. I silently cheer for him. I have never liked that old woman, and I am sympathetic to the plight of the hungry in our city. Things were not always this bad, but while the wealthy have prospered, their economic gain has not translated into an improved way of life for all. There seems to be a larger number of poor in the city than ever. Many are immigrants who do not qualify for free food from the city because they do not have the status of citizens. They are excluded from the guilds for the same reason and must make do as unskilled laborers. If anyone had reason to riot, it would surely be these people, who cannot feed their children though they live in the empire's wealthiest city.

There is much work still to be done back at the shop, so I reluctantly say goodbye to my friend and head for home with the goods from the market. As I walk by, I glance up at the city hall. Are the members of the council already huddled in their chamber, working on a religious settlement that will satisfy everyone and restore peace and unity to Augsburg? I hope so. I am tired of all the religious discord the past several years. Since all the educated priests and theologians and humanists can't seem to decide how the church should be run, perhaps our own eminently practical guildsmen, merchants, and patricians can figure it out.

BASIC FEATURES OF REACTING TO THE PAST

This is a historical role-playing game set in a moment of heightened historical tension; it places you in the role of a person from the period. After a few preparatory lectures, the game begins and the students are in charge. By reading the game book and your individual role sheet, you will find out more about your objectives, worldview, allies, and opponents. You must then attempt to achieve victory through formal speeches, informal debate, negotiations, and conspiracy. Outcomes sometimes differ from actual history; a debriefing session sets the record straight. What follows is an outline of what you will encounter in Reacting and what you will be expected to do.

Game Setup

Your instructor will spend some time before the beginning of the game helping you understand the historical context for the game. During the setup period, you will use several different kinds of material:

- The game book (what you are reading now), which includes historical information, rules and elements of the game, and essential historical documents.
- A role sheet, which provides a short biography of the historical person you will model in the game as well as that person's ideology, objectives, responsibilities, and resources. Some roles are based on historical figures. Others are "composites," with elements drawn from a number of individuals. You will receive your role sheet from your instructor.

Familiarize yourself with the documents before the game begins and return to them once you are in role. They contain information and arguments that will be useful as the game unfolds. A second reading while in role will deepen your understanding and alter your perspective. Once the game is in motion, your perspectives may change. Some ideas may begin to look quite different. Those who have carefully read the materials and who know the rules of the game will invariably do better than those who rely on general impressions and uncertain memories.

Game Play

Once the game begins, class sessions are run by students. In most cases, a single student serves as a sort of presiding officer. The instructor then becomes the GM (the "game master" or "game manager") and takes a seat in the back of the room. Though they do not lead the class sessions, GMs may do any of the following:

- Pass notes
- Announce important events
- Redirect proceedings that have gone off track

Instructors are, of course, available for consultations before and after game sessions. Although they will not let you in on any of the secrets of the game, they can be invaluable in terms of sharpening your arguments or finding key historical resources.

The presiding officer is expected to observe basic standards of fairness, but as a fail-safe device, most games employ the "podium rule," which allows a student who has not yet been recognized to approach the podium and wait for a chance to speak. Once at the podium, the student has the floor and must be heard.

Role sheets contain private, secret information that you must guard. Exercise caution when discussing your role with others. Your role sheet might identify likely allies, but even they may not always be trustworthy. However, keeping your own counsel and saying nothing to anyone is not an option. To achieve your objectives, you must speak with others. You will never muster the voting strength to prevail without allies. Collaboration and coalition building are at the heart of every game.

Some games feature strong alliances called factions. As a counterbalance, these games include roles called Indeterminates. They operate outside the established factions, and while some are entirely neutral, most possess their own idiosyncratic objectives. If you are in a faction, cultivating Indeterminates is in your interest, since they can be persuaded to support your position. If you are lucky enough to have drawn the role of an Indeterminate, you should be pleased; you will likely play a pivotal role in the outcome of the game.

Game Requirements

Students playing Reacting games practice persuasive writing, public speaking, critical thinking, teamwork, negotiation, problem solving, collaboration, adapting to changing circumstances, and working under pressure to meet deadlines. Your instructor will explain the specific requirements for your class. In general, though, a Reacting game asks you to perform three distinct activities:

Reading and writing. What you read can often be put to immediate use, and what you write is meant to persuade others to act the way you want them to. The reading load may vary slightly from role to role, and the writing requirement depends on your particular course. Papers are often policy statements, but they can also be autobiographies, battle plans, newspaper articles, poems, or after-game reflections. Papers often provide the foundation for the speeches delivered in class. They also help to familiarize you with the issues, which should allow you to ask good questions.

Public speaking and debate. In the course of a game, almost everyone is expected to deliver at least one formal speech from the podium (the length of the game and the size of the class will determine the number of speeches). Debate follows. It can be impromptu, raucous, and fast paced. At some point, discussions must lead to action, which often means proposing, debating, and passing a variety of resolutions. GMs may stipulate that students deliver their papers from memory when at the podium, or they may insist that students begin to wean themselves from dependency on written notes as the game progresses.

Wherever the game imaginatively puts you, it will surely not put you in the present. Accordingly, the colloquialisms and familiarities of today's college life are out of place. Never open your speech with a salutation like "Hi guys" when something like "Fellow citizens!" would be more appropriate.

Always seek allies to back your points when you are speaking at the podium. Do your best to have at least one supporter second your proposal, come to your defense, or admonish inattentive members of the body. Note-passing and side conversations, while common occurrences, will likely spoil the effect of your speech, so you and your supporters should insist on order before such behavior becomes too disruptive. Ask the presiding officer to assist you. Appeal to the GM as a last resort.

Strategizing. Communication among students is an essential feature of Reacting games. You will likely find yourself writing emails, texting, attending out-of-class meetings, or gathering for meals. The purpose of frequent communication is to lay out a strategy for achieving your objectives, thwarting your opponents, and hatching plots. When communicating with fellow students in or out of class, always assume that they are speaking to you in role. If you want to talk about the "real world," make that clear.

CONTROVERSY

Most Reacting games take place at moments of conflict in the past and therefore are likely to address difficult, even painful, issues that we continue to grapple with today. Consequently, this game may contain controversial subject matter. You may need to represent ideas with which you personally disagree or find repugnant. When speaking about these ideas, make it clear that you are speaking in role. Furthermore, if other people say things that offend you, recognize that they too are playing roles. If you decide to respond to them, do so using the voice of your role and make this clear. If these efforts are insufficient, or the ideas associated with your particular role seem potentially overwhelming, talk to your GM.

When playing your role, rely on your role sheet and the other game materials rather than drawing on caricature or stereotype. Do not use racial and ethnic slurs even if they are historically appropriate. If you are concerned about the potential for cultural appropriation or the use of demeaning language in your game, talk to your GM.

Amid the plotting, debating, and voting, always remember that this is an immersive role-playing game. Other players may resist your efforts, attack your ideas, and even betray a confidence. They take these actions because they are playing their roles. If you become concerned about the potential for game-based conflict to bleed out into the real world, take a step back and reflect on the situation. If your concerns persist, talk to your GM.

COUNTERFACTUALS

Every character in this game was a real historical person, and the biographical material presented reflects the best information we have from surviving documents in the Augsburg City Archives (Stadtarchiv Augsburg) about each person's life experiences and religious convictions. However, some of the characters in the game have had their lives artificially prolonged, and others have begun their tenure on the city council a few years early. For balance, some people who were historically members of the Gentlemen's Drinking Club will not begin the game as members of the club.

The "city council" represents Augsburg's forty-four-member Small Council (*kleiner Rat*), where most of the debates and decisions took place. Depending on the size of the class, some guilds may be represented by more than two members on the council. For the sake of simplicity, we have set aside the Large Council (*großer Rat*) and the executive Council of Thirteen (*Dreizehner*), which also contributed to the governance system of early sixteenth-century Augsburg. And we have condensed and focused the time frame of the Reformation debates, which took place from 1530 to 1537 when Augsburg's Church Order (*Kirchenordnung*) was finalized and established.

Authorities captured and interrogated suspected Anabaptist Agnes Vogel in 1528, but for convenience her testimony is grouped with the Nässlins and Ursula Germair, who were captured and interrogated in 1533.

2 Historical Background

BRIEF CHRONOLOGY OF THE EARLY REFORMATION

1517 Martin Luther publishes *95 Theses against Indulgences* and touches off the Reformation.

1518 Luther travels to Augsburg to meet with papal representative Cardinal **Cajetan**.

1520 Luther publishes three treatises: *On the Babylonian Captivity of the Church*, *Appeal to the Christian Nobility*, and *Freedom of a Christian*.

1521 Pope Leo X excommunicates Luther. Luther invited to meet with Charles V at the Diet of Worms; he refuses to recant his opinions and escapes to Wartburg Castle in Saxony.

1522 Luther publishes a German translation of the **New Testament**.

1524 The **Schilling** Revolt takes place in Augsburg, and the German Peasants' War begins.

1524 The Swiss city of Zurich becomes fully reformed under Ulrich Zwingli, and Zwingli marries Anna Reinhard.

1525 The rebellious peasants are massacred at Frankenhausen, ending the Peasants' War.

1525 Luther marries Katharina von Bora.

1529 Luther meets Ulrich Zwingli at Marburg but fails to come to an agreement on the meaning and practice of the Eucharist.

1530 Charles V calls for a Reichstag at Augsburg. **Philip Melanchthon** presents the *Augsburg Confession*, the church responds with the *Confutatio Pontificia*, and **Martin Bucer** offers the *Tetrapolitan Confession*.

1531 Zwingli dies in the Battle of Kappel.

Augsburg and the Reformation

With a population of approximately 30,000 in the early 1500s, Augsburg stood alongside Nuremberg and Cologne as one of the largest cities in all of central Europe. Wealthy and powerful, it attracted the finest artists and craftspeople and became a major center for early capitalism. Holy Roman Emperor Charles V became known as the "mayor of Augsburg" due to his frequent visits and long stays in the city. When the Reformation began in 1517, Augsburg stood in the center of religious debates throughout Europe and frequently hosted important meetings about the fate of reform. A variety of political, economic, social, and military factors complicated Augsburg's own reform process, which city authorities delayed as long as they could, allowing the city to host a smorgasbord of religious options in the meantime. It took the political pressure of the Imperial Reichstag of 1530 and continued religious chaos to convince the city council that they must, finally, decide on a unified set of religious practices for all the churches in the city to follow. Only then could Augsburg's citizens return to their primary interests: producing the finest goods for trade, making money, and spreading their influence throughout an expanding sixteenth-century world.

Augsburg in the Sixteenth Century

Augsburg's Roman founders situated the city in an ideal location: a fertile plain north of the Alps in a region known as Swabia. The Lech and Wertach Rivers, diverted into urban canals, provided abundant fresh water for a growing population and allowed for the extensive production of textiles and other goods that required flowing water. The Via Claudia, the ancient Roman road, ran through Augsburg, south to Venice, and north toward the Hanseatic cities and the Low Countries. These geographic advantages allowed Augsburg's family firms of craftsmen and merchants to transition from trade to finance work and thus amass enormous wealth in the fifteenth and sixteenth centuries. Augsburg's influence extended throughout Europe and the world; its wealthy merchant firms financed expeditions around the globe and established branches as far away as Venezuela and India.

Through a charter from the Holy Roman Emperor, Augsburg held the status of a "free imperial city" (*freie Reichstadt*), allowing self-governance as a semi-independent city-state under the jurisdiction of the emperor but not subject to any of the princes, dukes, or archbishops that governed the territories around it. Augsburg's constitution, established in 1368, revolved around the city's eighteen craft guilds. Most of Augsburg's citizens were connected to a guild, and each year guild members elected a guild master and other officials who would operate the guilds and represent them in city government. The eleven largest guilds sent both the current and immediate past guild masters as representatives to the Small Council; the seven smaller guilds sent only the current guild master. Once these representatives took their positions, they invited fifteen patricians—members of high-status noble families—to join them, bringing the total number of council members to forty-four. The council then elected two from its number, one guildsman and one patrician, to serve as mayors (*Burgermeister*) for the year. The council also appointed members to various other offices in city government.

The city council was meant to be broadly representative of the people through the guild elections, but in reality it was dominated by an oligarchy of wealthy elites: patricians, merchants, and bankers who wielded significant economic and social power. After their city council sessions, these men would frequently move across the street to the Gentlemen's Drinking Club (*Herrentrinkstube*), a social organization whose members included only the highest-status men in Augsburg. The most prominent member of the Gentlemen's Drinking Club was Jakob Fugger (pronounced FOO-ger), one of the richest men in Europe at the turn of the sixteenth century. The Fugger family started out as simple weavers in the fourteenth century, but smart business moves and advantageous marriages over several generations saw them abandon textile production to focus on the trading of textiles and other goods. By the early sixteenth century, the Fugger trading house oversaw enterprises as diverse as the spice trade, silver mining, and high finance. The Fugger bank lent money to popes, kings, and emperors. When Charles, the king of Spain, wished to become the Holy Roman Emperor in 1519, he borrowed money from Jakob

View of Augsburg, Germany. Colored woodcut by Michael Wohlgemut or Wilhelm Pleydenwurff. From Hartmann Schedel, *The Nuremberg Chronical* (1493). INTERFOTO / Alamy Stock Photo.

Fugger to bribe the **electors** and ensure his election, and Pope Leo X relied on Fugger credit to pay the mercenary Swiss Guards that protected the Vatican palace. After Jakob Fugger's death in 1525, his nephew Anton took over the family firm. Though they were far too busy to serve on the city council themselves, Jakob and Anton Fugger made their influence felt through their fellow merchant elites in the Gentlemen's Drinking Club.

To ensure its continued political independence and protect its growing wealth, Augsburg became part of an alliance known as the **Swabian League** (*Schwäbischer Bund*). This alliance was meant to keep the peace and protect the cities and territories of Swabia from the expansionist tendencies of neighboring principalities, especially the Duchy of Bavaria. Augsburg contributed funds to support the league's standing mercenary army of 12,000 infantrymen and 1,200 cavalry. In addition, Augsburg had its own city guard, which all male citizens were expected to serve in or support. Thick walls surrounded the city, which could only be accessed through carefully guarded gates. Inside the city, armories stored weapons and ammunition in case of emergency.

Unfortunately, the wealth flowing into Augsburg did not distribute itself equally among its inhabitants. A wide gap developed between the wealthy elites and the craftsmen, dayworkers, and immigrants that constituted most of Augsburg's population. While the rich merchant families built huge urban palaces in the latest Italian Renaissance style, the growing population of average Augsburgers lived in increasingly cramped and unhealthy quarters—if they were fortunate enough to find housing at all. Repeated attempts to exclude noncitizens hardly stemmed the tide of immigrants, and more and more people relied on free food provided by the city or the churches. Jakob Fugger attempted to remedy some of the problem by building the *Fuggerei*, a housing complex for the poor who would be expected to pay only nominal rent and pray daily for his soul. But even the construction of the *Fuggerei* did not lessen the resentment felt by many average Augsburgers toward their fellow citizens who basked in extravagant wealth.

Late Medieval Religion

At the turn of the sixteenth century, every person in Augsburg followed the same religion, just like practically everyone else in Europe. Western Europeans considered themselves part of a unified "Christendom" that looked to the pope in Rome as the head of the Christian church, established by Jesus Christ in the first century of the common era, and they recognized the pope's sole authority on all religious matters. People were vaguely aware of the existence of Orthodox Christians who followed the Bishop of Constantinople and lived alongside Muslims in the Ottoman Empire to the east, but most never interacted with those from other religious backgrounds unless they worked for a merchant house that regularly traveled to cosmopolitan port cities like Venice. The only non-Christians most people from Augsburg had ever met were Jews who lived in small communities outside the city walls and came into Augsburg during the day to trade. Though they generally had good relations with their Jewish neighbors, Augsburgers were proud of their communal identity as a unified Christian city worthy of God's special favor and protection. The inhabitants of Augsburg surely had differing levels of enthusiasm for the obligations of Christian practice, but they never questioned their identity as Christians. Alternate worldviews like atheism would not develop for a few more centuries, and conversion from Christianity to Judaism was unheard of, though Jews often faced strong pressure to convert to Christianity.

To administer a complex church that covered such a vast territory and population, the pope relied on cardinals and other high-church officials who lived in Rome and functioned as a quasi-political bureaucracy. These officials kept track of the rules and traditions of the church (known as **canon law**) and helped establish and enforce the pope's decrees. The church divided Europe into administrative units called **dioceses** which were each headed by a bishop or archbishop. A diocese might or might not conform to political boundaries; for example, the Bishop of Augsburg had spiritual responsibility over a large swath of territory outside the city and spent most of his time at the bishop's palace in the town of Dillingen, thirty miles (fifty kilometers) northeast of Augsburg. Bishops and archbishops lived like princes, receiving their income from tithes, offerings, and the rents from church-owned lands. In fact, many were actual princes. Noble families vied with each other and frequently paid money to have their younger sons placed in advantageous positions within the church, allowing them to live comfortably and perform favors for their noble friends and relatives.

The smallest administrative unit of the church was the parish. Augsburg had six parishes, each with a dedicated parish church. On the southern end of the city stood the Basilica of Sts. Ulrich and Afra, which housed a monastery of Benedictine **monks** but also served as a parish church for those in the neighborhood. The Church of St. Moritz in the center of town served as the parish for many elite merchant and patrician families. To the east, the Franciscan church (also known as the *Barfüßer* for its barefoot Franciscan friars) stood right along the inner wall that separated the older sections of the city from St. Jakob's quarter, where many weavers and poorer citizens lived. The Church of St. Stephen anchored a parish in the northeast corner of Augsburg, and the Augustinian **canons** at St. Georg and Holy Cross served the northern and northwestern sections of the city. The monks, canons, and friars who served in Augsburg's parishes lived in their own separate houses, dressed similarly, and ordered their lives according to a particular set of "rules." For example, the friars who staffed the Franciscan church followed the Rule of St. Francis, which included a vow of poverty and a promise to serve the needy. The monks at Sts. Ulrich and Afra lived regimented lives according to the Rule of St. Benedict and spent more time in their monastery—either at work or in prayer—and less time out in the public streets of Augsburg. Despite the particularities of their various orders, all were set apart from larger society due to their special role as ordained **clergy**.

Augsburg had many other churches and religious buildings aside from those specifically designated as parishes. Most notably, the Cathedral Church of Our Lady, the oldest and largest church in the city, was under the direct control of the Bishop of Augsburg, with his official city residence standing alongside it. Nearby were also cloisters housing the cathedral canons—priests of high status who came from noble and patrician families outside of Augsburg. A Carmelite monastery dedicated to St. Anna occupied the western edge of the city. Augsburg was home to two large convents of nuns, mostly the unmarried daughters of wealthy noble or patrician families, who resided together in the secluded but luxurious convents of St. Katherine and St. Margaret. There were even a few small chapels built for specific purposes, such as the Chapel of the Holy Ghost in the hospital and the Church of St. Jakob that housed pilgrims on their way to San Juan de Compostela in Spain.

Late medieval Augsburg was proud of its beautiful churches and chapels. As Augsburg's wealth grew, so did donations of money and land, along with paintings, statues, rich textiles, fine gold objects, stained glass windows, and massive, ornate altars. Jakob Fugger brought craftsmen from Italy to build his family their own Renaissance-style memorial chapel on the west end of St. Anna's church; the "Fugger Chapel" is the first example of Italianate architecture north of the Alps. The guild of goldsmiths pooled their funds to build another chapel onto the north side of the same church where they could meet and pray together as guildsmen. The neighboring dukes of Bavaria gave many generous gifts to the Benedictine Monastery of Sts. Ulrich and Afra and visited frequently. From the wealthiest nobleman to the lowliest day worker, people in and around Augsburg poured money into the churches in hopes that after death their donations would demonstrate their worthiness to enter heaven, or at the very least, shorten the time they would have to spend working off their sins in **purgatory**.

A church was a place of wonder and miracles, a holy space that allowed a person to temporarily leave the realities of daily life and contemplate the heavenly realm. One could leave the dirty, smelly, crowded streets of Augsburg and walk through the doors of a church into a place of quiet contemplation. Thick stone walls muffled noise from the world outside. Soft light filtered through stained glass and flickered from candles, where the scent of wax and tallow mingled with incense. In the church, one could view or participate in the **sacraments**: ritual actions that brought the powers of heaven down to earth. Near the church doors stood a font of water

Hans Holbein the Younger, *Death and the Preacher (Totentanz)*, 1523–25. Wikimedia Commons.

where infants could be purified and cleansed of Adam and Eve's **original sin** through **baptism**. Older children experienced the sacrament of **confirmation**, and later in life might be joined in **marriage** or set apart as a member of the clergy through **ordination**. All Christians were expected to regularly confess their sins, perform acts of **penance**, and receive **absolution**. They could peek through a screen separating the public space of the church from the holy space around the altar and watch a priest murmur in Latin as he transformed the **wafer** and wine of the **Eucharist** into the literal body and blood of Jesus Christ. Of the late medieval church's seven sacraments, only **anointing** (last rites) was not regularly performed in a church building.

The church could also be a place of learning. Parishioners brought folding chairs from home or stood around the pulpit to hear the preaching of a sermon or the explanation of a passage from the

HISTORICAL BACKGROUND 13

Bible. Even half a century after the invention of Gutenberg's printing press, very few people had the literacy level and wealth necessary to own and read a Bible themselves. Even fewer could understand Latin, the language of the Christian Bible. So they relied on the priest to read them the words of God and explain their meaning. And they relied even more on the work of artists and craftspeople, who created visual images that emphasized stories, doctrines, or figures from the Bible or church history. More attuned to visual cues than words, any visitor to a church could readily identify the twelve apostles, biblical prophets, and important **saints**, especially those to whom the church was dedicated. They recognized the melancholy maternal love of the Virgin Mary and the redemptive agony of the crucified Christ. They saw images of demons and the horrors of purgatory and hell so they would know what fate awaited them if they died without sufficiently resolving their sins.

In theory, all these churches, chapels, and religious institutions fell under the jurisdiction of the Bishop of Augsburg, who answered directly to the pope in Rome. In practice, however, powerful religious orders like the Benedictines and the Augustinians operated their monasteries in relative independence. And secular authorities like the city council, important families, and big donors exercised significant influence in how churches were staffed and run. Having an interest in the religious discipline of the city, Augsburg's city council took increasing control over traditional church functions like poor relief, and they hired charismatic clergymen to exhort the people to obedience and righteous living. Individual parishes elected **laymen** (nonclergy) from the community to oversee the finances of the parish churches and ensure donations were being used properly. Educated men like Augsburg's council clerk Conrad Peutinger collected the writings of prominent theologians and humanists like **Desiderius Erasmus** and Thomas á Kempis, engaging in discussions about how to live a more spiritual life and address problems within the church. From the top to the bottom of society, regular people took a strong interest in the doctrines and functions of the church, effectively limiting the unchecked power of church authorities—even the office of the pope.

The Reformation Comes to Augsburg, 1517–1524

In the spring of 1517, the Bishop of Augsburg, Christoph von Stadion, began introducing reforms to the church in his diocese. The bishop, a smart man with a humanist education, had read the writings of Erasmus and knew firsthand the structural problems within the church. Unfortunately, the bishop's plan for internal reform came too late. On October 31 of the same year, an Augustinian friar in Wittenberg named Martin Luther wrote *95 Theses against the Sale of Indulgences* in hopes of provoking a debate about the church's approach to saving souls. Passing from printer to printer, these bold statements from an obscure theologian reached Augsburg within a few weeks and immediately caused a stir. The bishop's plans for gradual, top-down reform of the diocese of Augsburg soon gave way to insistent popular demands for a major reevaluation of the church's structure, doctrines, and practices, all ignited by Luther's challenge.

Luther wrote his *95 Theses* in response to the church's practice of offering indulgences; that is, the promise of forgiveness from sin in exchange for money. Half of the funds raised through the sale of indulgences in Wittenberg went to pay the debts of the Archbishop of Mainz, Luther's superior in the church, who had borrowed money from the Fugger family of Augsburg to purchase his church office. The remaining money went to Rome, where Pope Leo X was in the process of expanding his palace and building a massive new church in honor of St. Peter, thanks to generous lines of credit from Augsburg's bankers. Martin Luther had been to Rome and seen the pope's ambitious building projects in person. He went there during a crisis of faith in 1512, hoping that a pilgrimage to the holiest sites in Europe would help him feel assured of his own salvation. His trip had the opposite effect, leaving him disillusioned about the leadership of the church. After returning to Witten-

Workshop of Lucas Cranach the Elder, *Martin Luther as an Augustinian Monk*, after 1546. Wikimedia Commons.

berg, Luther still suffered under a crippling fear that he would end up in hell, feeling himself too profound a sinner to gain admission to heaven.

One night, as he read the Bible and brooded over his fate, Martin Luther had what became known as his "tower experience." Reading in Romans 1:17 that the righteous live by faith, Luther decided that a person could not be released from sin by doing **works** like going on pilgrimages, performing the sacraments, donating treasures to the church, or buying indulgences. Rather, salvation must come through faith alone (*sola fide*). Worried that as a sinner he might not have enough faith, Luther concluded that **grace** alone (*sola gratia*) made him capable of faith, and this grace was given to him by God regardless of his worthiness. Luther determined that the ultimate authority for Christian practice came from scripture alone (*sola scriptura*), not from the decisions of the pope or his officials. So when representatives of the pope and the Archbishop of Mainz came to Wittenberg selling indulgences to Luther's parishioners in exchange for the promise of salvation, Luther had arguments ready—arguments that received a surprisingly enthusiastic response from common people throughout Europe.

Luther did not stop with the *95 Theses*. The more other clergymen challenged his ideas, the harder he pushed back. Within a few months, even Rome had heard about the defiant friar in Wittenberg. In 1518, Pope Leo X called Martin Luther to Augsburg to meet with his representative, Cardinal Cajetan. Luther made the 300-mile (500 kilometers) journey from Wittenberg to Augsburg on foot and lodged with the Carmelites at St. Anna's monastery. The abbot of St. Anna, **Johann Frosch**, quickly became a strong supporter of Luther, and the monks of St. Anna likewise became the first and most stalwart "Lutherans" of Augsburg. But not everyone was similarly convinced. Conrad Peutinger invited Luther to dinner and engaged him in several long conversations. Peutinger was sympathetic to Luther on many points but found his challenges to papal authority dangerous and potentially destabilizing. When Luther finally met with Cardinal Cajetan in the sumptuous palace of Anton Fugger, it did not go well at all. Luther refused to accede to the church's demands that he recant his opinions, and Cajetan would not hear Luther's arguments about the need to reform church doctrines. Both men departed Augsburg dissatisfied, but not without leaving a lasting impact on the city's trajectory of religious reform.

In the months following Martin Luther's visit to Augsburg, preachers in some of the city's churches began advocating a reformed practice of the sacraments. The Fugger family attempted to stop the preacher at St. Moritz church, Johann Speiser, from speaking to congregants about reformed ideas, but the laymen overseeing the parish protected Speiser and allowed him to continue. A new preacher hired to work in the cathedral, **Urbanus Rhegius**, quickly showed similar reformist tendencies, but the cathedral chapter was afraid to remove him because of the people's strong support. In 1522, the city council passed an ordinance declaring that only deserving Augsburg citizens could beg on the streets or receive free food. This was partly meant to discourage the many migrants coming from outside the city, but also partly a power grab by the city to blunt the authority of the Bishop of Augsburg who traditionally oversaw all poor relief in his diocese. The bishop was no more able to prevent the council's encroachment on his authority than he was able to get rid of Speiser, Frosch, or Rhegius. Luther's questioning of the pope's authority made the power of all church officials vulnerable.

Back in Wittenberg, Luther continued to speak and write furiously. In the fall of 1520, he released three important treatises on religious reform. *The Babylonian Captivity of the Church* argued that the Bible contains evidence of only two, not seven, sacraments: baptism and the Eucharist. *The Freedom of a Christian* presented an alternate vision of how to live a Christian life that centered on the agency of the individual. *To the Christian Nobility of the German Nation* urged the princes and other secular authorities to unite and force the church to reform. Calling him "a wild boar in the forest," Pope Leo X excommunicated Luther in January 1521; Luther responded in typical incendiary fashion by calling the pope an Antichrist. The newly elected Holy Roman Emperor Charles V hoped to quell the growing controversy in his empire by summoning Luther to an imperial assembly (a diet) planned in the city of Worms in the spring of 1521. Luther again walked over 300 miles (500 kilometers) from Wittenberg to Worms to answer the emperor's order, but even in the face of imperial power and majesty Luther remained as defiant as ever. For his own safety, he went into hiding at Wartburg Castle in Saxony, where he ensconced himself in a room and translated the Bible's New Testament from Greek and Latin into vernacular German. Of all Luther's publications, his September 1522 release of a German Bible was the most signifi-

Christoph Amberger, *Conrad Peutinger*, 1543.
Alto Vintage Images / Alamy Stock Photo.

cant. Now, even those unable to read the Bible themselves could hear it read to them, resulting in the church losing its interpretive control of the text.

Meanwhile, other visions for church reform had begun to take hold, some of which went far beyond Luther's. The Swiss priest Ulrich (or Huldrych) Zwingli had also condemned the sale of indulgences in 1517; however, unlike in Luther's case, Zwingli's bishop found the arguments convincing and ordered the practice to cease in his diocese with little public fanfare. Zwingli continued to agitate for reform, and in 1522 he seized the spotlight from Luther by advocating for an end to **fasting** during Lent, the forty-day period preceding Easter during which Christians traditionally abstained from eating meat and other animal products. Other reformers soon emerged in towns and villages across the Holy Roman Empire. Some supported the church reform visions advocated by Luther or Zwingli, but many took these ideas

Hans Asper, *Portrait of Ulrich Zwingli*, 1549. Wikimedia Commons.

in a different direction, with some advocating a much more thorough and radical reform of the church than either Zwingli or Luther were comfortable with. The pope also had his defenders; notably, the priest and theologian **Johann Maier von Eck**, who was one of the first to push back against Luther's challenge in 1517 and continued to champion the traditions of the institutional church through the 1520s.

By 1523, Augsburg was awash in incendiary propaganda pamphlets, produced by local printers for wide distribution, reflecting all sides of these religious questions. Concerned that religious conflict might spill over into physical violence, Augsburg's city council brought all the printers in the city together for a meeting and required them to swear they would not print anything without permission from council clerk Peutinger. A few printers took strategic vacations to miss the meeting. But those that attended ignored the new rules, and the council did not enforce them, even after Luther's former associate Andreas Karlstadt published a controversial pamphlet radically redefining the Eucharist, kicking off a controversy in Augsburg and elsewhere about the meaning and performance of the sacraments. Augsburg's cathedral preacher Urbanus Rhegius published a moderate rebuttal to Karlstadt, leading to a drop in support from Augsburg citizens who were already pushing for more radical reforms. The cathedral chapter took advantage of Rhegius's weakness and fired him from his position as preacher. But this did not prevent continued problems for the Bishop of Augsburg. Increasingly, people followed Zwingli and flouted the Lenten fasts by openly eating sausage, thereby affirming their support for reform and defying traditions of the church they argued did not have a clear scriptural basis. Zwingli declared priestly **celibacy** similarly unjustified by the Bible and married the widow Anna Reinhard in 1524. Dozens of Augsburg priests followed his example in the subsequent two years, including Urbanus Rhegius. Martin Luther came to the same conclusion regarding the church's tradition of priestly celibacy; he supported these weddings and himself married a former nun, Katharina von Bora, in 1525.

Although Luther was the first major reformer whose ideas reached Augsburg, Zwingli and the Swiss reformers quickly became the most popular, especially among the lower-class craftspeople and workers. This might be because the Swiss reformers offered a more thorough reform than the relatively moderate Wittenbergers, and the people wanted sweeping change. It might be because the Swiss reformers appealed to a communitarian spirit, whereas Luther looked to the authority of dukes and princes to establish reform. Or perhaps the Swiss vision for religious reform simply resonated more strongly with the people. Whatever the reason, many Augsburgers began to gravitate toward preachers influenced by Zwingli, demand opportunities to hear the preachers of their choice, and participate in reformed sacraments. In 1526, two apprentices were caught trespassing in the garden of the bishop's residence and boldly

Daniel Hopfer, *Moresca Dancers Surrounding a Sausage Seller*, 1523. Wikimedia Commons.

declared that they intended to take the space to build a new church in order to hear the "clean and pure word of God." Within a few months, the elected lay financial custodians in charge of the parishes of St. Ulrich, St. George, and Holy Cross added their "preaching chapels" to the churches of St. Anna, St. Moritz, and the Franciscans as places where inhabitants of Augsburg could hear reformed preaching and practice reformed rituals. Since there were so many competing ideas about how the church ought to be reformed, Augsburg's city council decided not to interfere in these developments, passively allowing a variety of reforming groups to become established, while hoping that the Roman church and its theologians would quickly sort out which reforms would return the Christian church to unity.

Reformation Radicalism, 1524–1530

In the spring of 1524, the Franciscan friar Johann Schilling arrived in Augsburg to take a city-funded preaching position at the Franciscan church. His preaching was more extreme than any of the other reformers in Augsburg. He preached that all property should be held in common and that wealth should be redistributed from the rich to the poor. He advocated the kind of communion service described by Luther's former colleague Karlstadt, with the priest speaking in German and distributing both the wafer and the wine to congregants. He verbally attacked the city council, declaring that if the council refused to act in accordance with the will of the people, the people should replace the council. His sermons drew huge crowds, and Schilling quickly became the most popular preacher in Augsburg.

The city council members faced a dilemma. They knew that to defend the authority and interests of the

Bishop of Augsburg and the institutional church would lead to serious unrest among those who wanted change. On the other hand, openly defying the church would strain relations with the emperor and the Swabian League, imperiling Augsburg's lucrative trade monopolies and important military alliances. So the city council followed what they called a "middle way," remaining carefully and officially neutral on religious questions, tolerating various reformers without granting them any kind of official sanction. But Schilling was becoming a problem. His criticism of the city council's studied neutrality made it increasingly difficult for them to avoid the pressure from all sides that demanded a firm position on religious questions. Worse yet, some disturbing events had taken place since Schilling's arrival in town. Religious images in the cathedral cemetery were covered in cow's blood in an act of symbolic **iconoclasm**. A crucifix was stolen from the Church of the Holy Cross and desecrated. And then, in the summer of 1524, a group of weavers accosted an innocent monk in the Franciscan church who was attempting to consecrate holy water. Schilling was rumored to have planned these attacks. Whether or not that was true, the council had good reason to believe he inspired them. And there were other nasty rumors circulating about Schilling's interests and activities.

Secretly, a group of city council members met with Johann Schilling. They offered him twenty gold coins and a fast horse if he would quietly leave town. Schilling immediately accepted their offer, but he did not remain quiet. Soon, all the people of Augsburg knew the city council was to blame for their favorite preacher's sudden departure. During the council meeting on August 6, 1524, someone looked out the window and discovered that hundreds of people had begun to gather on the square outside the council house to demand the return of Johann Schilling. The crowd quickly swelled to as many as 1,800 people, who presented the city council with a list of demands that included the reinstatement of Schilling, a repeal of excise taxes on beer, limitations on the power of the clergy, and the release of a popular local prisoner.

The city council had little with which to defend itself militarily. A weapons arsenal existed deep within the St. Jakob's quarter, where the weavers lived. Most of the rioters in the streets were weavers. The town's cannons were stored in the Holy Cross quarter, another relatively poor and radicalized section of the city. The town guard could be activated if needed, but as it was made up of citizens who were usually mustered to defend Augsburg against invaders, it is unclear the extent to which it would be useful in an internal civic uprising. The only immediate defense for the council was a small troop of mercenary soldiers paid by the city council and currently ranged around the exterior of the city hall to keep the rioters at bay.

The council, led by mayor Hieronymus Imhof, announced the appointment of local reformer Urbanus Rhegius to the vacant preacher position, optimistic that this would quell the crowd. Imhof reportedly encouraged the council with these words: "My Lords and fellow councilmen, put all your fears aside, for our people are too obedient and pious to do anything to the council. So be of good cheer!" (See Clemens Sender's "Chronicle" in B. Ann Tlusty, ed., *Augsburg during the Reformation Era: An Anthology of Sources* [Indianapolis: Hackett, 2012], 8.) However, the appointment of a preacher the crowd considered insufficiently stalwart in reform did not satisfy them, and their anger continued to grow. Left with little choice, the council agreed to bring Johann Schilling back and sent Conrad Peutinger to tell the crowd they could have their preacher, provided they went home peacefully. After some further clamor, the crowd dispersed.

The popular uprising shook the council to its core. A few nights later, the council secretly ordered all the mercenary soldiers under their command to gather fully armed at six in the morning at the city hall and Gentlemen's Drinking Club to take a new oath to protect and defend the council. A few weeks later, the council ordered the beheading of two sixty-year-old weavers they accused of masterminding the rebellion: Hans Kag and Hans Speiser. A weaver's wife named Anna Fassnacht, who was overheard expressing support for the rebellion and frustration with the council, was banished from Augsburg for life. The council's swift reaction and strict justice reestablished their authority, but these events also taught them a lesson about the power of the crowd. Imhof's optimistic sense of the people as "obedient and pious" could not be relied on. The people took religious matters very seriously and were willing to rebel against their own civic leaders to protect what they saw as their right to worship in a way they deemed proper and to follow the preachers they approved of. The council quietly increased the number of mercenary soldiers under their control even as they knew the professionals would be outmatched if the crowd became implacable.

Concerns about the volatility of the common people became even more acute over the following months, as peasants in the Augsburg countryside revolted against their noble landlords with demands similar to those of the pro-Schilling protestors. Inspired by the teachings of radical reforming preachers like Thomas Münzer, the peasants wanted the right to choose their own pastors. They wanted greater freedom to hunt, fish, and gather firewood. They wanted limitations on the power of their feudal overlords. And they demanded to be treated with equality, just as Luther's Bible says they should. Martin Luther reacted with horror to the peasants' invocation of his ideas, writing *Against the Robbing and Murdering Hordes of Peasants* and reiterating the need for strict obedience to political authorities. Nevertheless, tens of thousands of peasants in Swabia and other rural areas of the Holy Roman Empire massed for war. Augsburg's city council gave the Swabian League extra funds to help put down the peasants' rebellion. The peasants were no match for heavily armed and trained professional fighters; the beginning of the end of the German Peasants' War came at the Battle of Frankenhausen in Thuringia on May 15, 1525, where the peasant fighters were massacred and Münzer was executed.

Augsburg's city council continued its carefully balanced stance on religious matters in the years following the Schilling uprising and the German Peasants' War, even as hopes dimmed for a quick resolution to the conflict over reform. Supporters of the pope defended church traditions and the established processes for making changes to church procedures by calling councils. But Martin Luther, Ulrich Zwingli, and other would-be reformers continued to preach, write, and publish, consolidating their positions and attracting allies among princes, clergy, and common people. On some issues, like the meaning and practice of the Eucharist, reformers continued to offer very different points of view. Luther and the Wittenberg reformers wanted to make a few changes in the way the sacrament was performed, for example, having the prayers said in German and the wine made available to common people alongside the wafer. They maintained a strong belief in the traditional church teaching that God, in the person of Jesus Christ, was truly present in the elements of the Eucharist. Zwingli and the Swiss reformers thought this did not go far enough, however, arguing that God's presence in the Eucharist had symbolic rather than literal meaning. Hoping to bring all reformers to agreement on this issue, the reformer Martin Bucer and Prince Philip of Hesse brought Luther and Zwingli together in the town of Marburg in October 1529. The meeting was a disaster. Though they agreed on many things, the Wittenberg and Swiss contingents could not reach consensus on the issue of whether God was present in the Eucharist. Both sides left in a huff, and Luther declared that it would be better for a person to attend a Roman-style **Mass** than a Swiss reformed service. The church reform movement remained divided, unable to articulate a unified alternative to the practices of the Roman church.

Meanwhile, people continued to read or listen to Luther's Bible translation and come to their own conclusions about what it meant. Many felt inspired to try living as the original followers of Jesus did, and they noted that many of the practices advocated by the traditional Roman church and mainstream reformers did not actually appear in the Bible. For

Philip Melanchthon Administers the Sacrament of Baptism. Detail of the Wittenberg Reformation altarpiece by Lucas Cranach the Elder, 1547, in the Stadtkirche St. Marien, Wittenberg. Lucas Cranach d.J.–Reformationsaltar, St. Marien zu Wittenberg, linker Flügel. The Picture Art Collection / Alamy Stock Photo.

example, the early Christians seem to have set themselves apart from the rest of society. They did not meet in fancy churches or have professional priests. People joined the community as adults through baptism, rather than performing baptism on infants who had no choice in the matter. Sixteenth-century Christians who attempted to worship in this strictly biblical way became known as Anabaptists, or Re-baptizers (*Wiedertäufer*). They met together in private homes or outdoor spaces, read the Bible together, and welcomed new members into their community through adult baptism. But this was such a radical departure from common Christian practice that it made religious and civic leaders very nervous. Because Anabaptists did not meet in churches, it was impossible for authorities to monitor and control what they taught. Refusing to baptize their infants meant there were children running around still tainted with original sin, which traditionalists and reformers agreed imperiled the children's souls and posed a danger to society. Anabaptists also refused to swear oaths or participate in civic respon-

Lambert Sustris (formerly attributed to Titian), *Emperor Charles V*, 1548. Wikimedia Commons.

sibilities like government or the town militia, preferring to remain apart from sinful society as much as possible. The Roman church and the various mainstream reforming movements did not agree on much, but they did agree that Anabaptists were dangerous radicals who must be stopped. By the late 1520s, Augsburg's city council felt compelled to intervene and stop the growth of Anabaptism in the city by arresting, exiling, or even executing Anabaptists who refused to recant their beliefs.

The Augsburg Reichstag of 1530

Holy Roman Emperor Charles V chose Augsburg as the location for his 1530 Reichstag, or imperial council. Charles planned to bring all the major princes and clergy of the empire together to finally solve the bothersome church reform conflicts once and for all, especially in light of other important issues such as the Ottoman military threat. The location was convenient for Charles, since his Fugger bankers lived in Augsburg and owned urban palaces grand enough to host such distinguished personages as himself and his entourage.

The people of Augsburg were less than excited about the impending Reichstag. Many guests would be coming to the city, which meant that there would be a shortage of housing, and food supplies would be tight, driving up prices. The festive atmosphere of these great congresses meant that the visitors would be drinking heavily and frequently behaving in an unruly manner, leading to resentment and conflict with the local population. And then there were the religious issues. Augsburg's city council continued its "middle way" policy, allowing the preaching of various reforming doctrines and the establishment of reformed churches, while also supporting traditional Roman church practices throughout the city. Charles knew about the religious diversity developing in Augsburg and determined to clamp down on it during his Reichstag. His representatives came before the city council brandishing the imperial charter, an implicit warning that Augsburg's status as a free imperial city with independent rights could be revoked at the emperor's will. Charles demanded that all professional soldiers in the employ of the Augsburg city council be dismissed for the duration of the Reichstag and replaced with 2,000 members of his own mercenary guard. To help support the emperor's guard, the council would be required to contribute the sum of 2,000 gold coins. Furthermore, the council must dismiss all pastors, preachers, or priests who did not follow the traditional form of the Mass or taught other "reformed" doctrines, and the council must also require all of Augsburg's citizens to attend the traditional Roman Mass during the Reichstag.

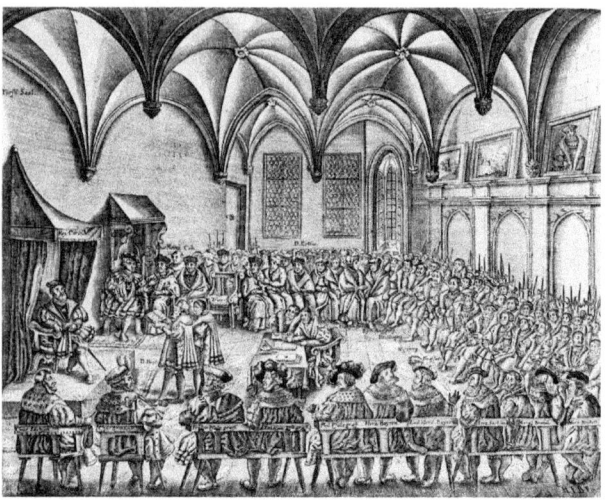

Karl Remshard, *Augsburg Confession*, 1708. Wikimedia Commons.

The council knew that to give in to these demands would spark a riot, and one which they could not call in their own soldiers to quell. They offered a compromise, dismissing some of their professional guard and contributing a smaller sum toward the upkeep of Charles's forces. They informed all the clergy in Augsburg that if they remained during the Reichstag they must refrain from preaching on controversial subjects, including the nature of the Eucharist. Some reform-minded preachers refused to abide by the restrictions and left the city, but many stayed.

The emperor made a triumphal entry into Augsburg on Corpus Christi Day in early June 1530 and officially began the Reichstag. Religious questions were first on the agenda. Martin Luther feared for his safety if he attended the Reichstag, so he sent his Wittenberg colleague Philip Melanchthon to represent his views. On June 25, Melanchthon presented the emperor with a list of religious issues on which the Wittenberg camp refused to compromise. This document, known as the *Augsburg Confession*, was the first comprehensive statement of Lutheran beliefs. Since there were several points of disagreement between Luther and the Swiss reformers, soon thereafter another document was presented to the emperor: the *Tetrapolitan Confession*. Written largely by

Martin Bucer, the *Tetrapolitan Confession* outlined the Swiss reformed position espoused by followers of Zwingli and supported by the four cities of Strasbourg, Lindau, Memmingen, and Constance. Eventually, Catholic clergy responded to these statements by issuing the *Confutatio Pontificia*, reaffirming the traditional positions of the Roman church. But by then, all attempts at religious conversation and compromise had already failed.

Meanwhile, some Augsburg preachers violated their agreement to avoid controversial preaching. Johann Schneider, a radical pastor at the preaching house of the Holy Cross, gave an incendiary sermon about the Eucharist in which he accused traditionalist clergy of "crucifying Christ anew" each time they celebrated the Mass. Schneider was arrested and imprisoned. A crowd of weavers attempted to storm the tower where he was held, but Charles's soldiers drove them back. To prevent further unrest, Schneider was quietly allowed to escape, and most other reforming clergy left the city as well. Charles, incensed by the Augsburg and Tetrapolitan confessions and the actions of the Augsburgers, demanded the restoration of the traditional Roman Mass to all Augsburg churches. He sent his soldiers to remove the newly installed pews in the Franciscan church, which was most closely aligned with Swiss reform. Fighting broke out between Spanish soldiers and parishioners, and the building was locked to prevent more disorder. Charles approached the council and offered to use his soldiers to restore traditional practices of religion in Augsburg by force. The council quickly rejected the offer but agreed to uphold Charles's authority and protect the clergy in the city who remained loyal to Rome.

The emperor and his entourage finally left Augsburg on November 23, 1530, having failed to achieve the religious concord everyone had hoped for. Instead, the Augsburg Reichstag hardened the resolve of various camps of reformers and led to the creation of three specific and mutually exclusive statements about the proper organization and practices of the Christian church. Furthermore, the events of the Reichstag made the members of Augsburg's city council finally realize that they could not keep up their "middle way" position any longer. With the church in turmoil, Augsburg needed to figure out how to reunify itself under a single, consistent set of religious practices that would apply to all the city's churches and clergy. This decision would not be without consequences. For practical as well as religious reasons, Conrad Peutinger and many of Augsburg's merchants wanted to keep Charles V happy and Augsburg's valuable monopolies safe by returning to traditional religious practices and supporting the pope in Rome. But many of the craftspeople and weavers of Augsburg had become convinced that the church needed a thorough reform and advocated a Swiss-style reformation. Wittenberg's vision for reform, as articulated in the *Augsburg Confession*, took a moderate position between the two poles but satisfied almost nobody. Augsburg city council members knew that whatever church ordinance they ultimately decided on would have to find a way to placate either the emperor or the people, and they would have to seek allies of a similar religious point of view to protect Augsburg from retribution. The guild masters and patricians of Augsburg's city council resolved to address the important issue of religion in Augsburg once and for all.

3
The Game

MAJOR ISSUES FOR DEBATE

As members of the city council of Augsburg in 1530, it is now your task to resolve the religious controversies within the city and establish military alliances that can protect Augsburg's economic and political interests. The conflicts during the 1530 Reichstag underline the necessity of establishing a set of official religious practices that could be approved and supported by the city council. Augsburg has lived in uncertainty long enough and has allowed theological divisions to disrupt the unity and economic growth of the city. Now the city council must determine what religious practices should take place in Augsburg. Can priests marry and people eat sausage during Lent? What should the churches look like? How should the sacraments be performed? What should be done about Anabaptists? The choices you make in these areas will affect the alliances Augsburg is able to secure, as well as the reactions of Emperor Charles V and the restless population of the city.

This is an exciting time in history. Old assumptions about religious practices are being questioned, and many new ideas are being tested for the first time. But note that everyone expects that the Christian church will eventually figure out what practices are right and return to its previous state of unity. The different factions in Augsburg's city council do not represent different religious denominations like "Lutheran" or "Catholic"; rather, they offer different approaches to the question of how the universal Christian church should fix its problems and move forward. As you debate these issues, keep in mind that religious doctrines develop and change over time, so modern understandings of these religious concepts may be very different from those of the 1530s. With a historical mindset, try to approach these ideas as the city council of Augsburg understood them.

Issue 1: "Sola Scriptura": Should Priests Be Allowed to Marry?

Shocked authorities levied a fine on attendees to the priest Jakob Griessbeutel's wedding in 1523 (including several city council members!), but in the following years, several other prominent Augsburg priests publicly married, led by the examples of Martin Luther and Ulrich Zwingli. Proponents of clerical marriage argue that Jesus supported marriage; after all, his first miracle involved procuring wine for a wedding feast (see John 2:1-10). But the traditions of the church have long followed Paul's admonition that celibacy is preferable to marriage (see 1 Cor. 7:9) and that priests, monks, and nuns as representatives of the church should remain celibate so they can focus on their ministry without being distracted by the needs of a family.

This issue comes down to whether Augsburg will follow canon law—the traditions of the church that require celibacy of priests—or reject canon law in favor of a literal reading of scripture, which does not appear to outright prohibit marriage. Priestly marriage was the first major application of reformers' claims that church practices should rely on "scripture alone" (*sola scriptura*) whenever there is a question about proper church practice. But the Bible is somewhat ambiguous on this issue. Can relying on scripture alone really provide enough direction about how the Christian church should operate?

Suggested Core Texts

The Augsburg Confession, Article XXIII
The Confutatio Pontificia, Defense to Article XXIII
Zwingli, *Of the Clarity and Certainty of the Word of God*
Eck, *Enchiridion of Commonplaces and Articles on the New Teachings*, Chapters 11, 19
Melanchthon, *Apology of the Augsburg Confession*, Article XXIII

Scriptural Sources

New Testament: Luke 20:34-35; John 2:3-10; 1 Corinthians 7; Timothy 4:1-3

Additional Sources

"Description of a Priestly Marriage" and "Urbanus Rhegius, a Sermon about Marriage," in B. Ann Tlusty, ed., *Augsburg during the Reformation Era: An Anthology of Sources* (Indianapolis: Hackett, 2012), 95-99.

Issue 2: Faith versus Works: Should Augsburg's Citizens Be Punished for Eating Meat on Lenten Fast Days?

For the period of Lent—the forty days before Easter—Christian tradition of the sixteenth century prescribes complete abstention from meat and animal products such as dairy and eggs. People are also expected to fast—go without food entirely—on certain days. But reformers argue that there is no scriptural basis for this tradition and that "works" such as fasting have no impact on salvation. For Augsburgers who favor reform, a popular show of resistance to church authority involves eating sausage during Lent. The pungent scent of cooking sausage easily spreads throughout the house and into the street as an unmistakable and public demonstration of resistance through the private act of preparing food. Zwingli kicked off the Reformation in Zurich in 1522 by preaching against Lent and then, reportedly, feasting on sausages at the home of a supporter. The consumption of any meat during Lent—especially strong-smelling, inexpensive sausage—is a provocative act that could disrupt the peace and unity of the Augsburg community.

Like clerical marriage, the consumption of meat during Lent is an issue pitting the church traditions of canon law against the literal word of scripture, which says nothing about Lent, though it does report that Jesus endured a forty-day fast (see Matthew 4:1-4). But for many ordinary people, the requirements of the Lenten fast represent all the onerous requirements and "works" the church requires of them. If the reformers are right and salvation is an unmerited gift, then abstaining from meat during Lent would have no impact on whether a person would go to heaven. A person's faith alone (*sola fide*), obtained through grace alone (*sola gratia*), determines their salvation irrespective of any works they might perform. On the other hand, following traditions such as abstaining from meat during Lent can be a demonstration of a person's faith, since "faith without works is dead" (James 2:17). And even the reform-minded had reason to fear the social instability that could result from offensive, inflammatory, and rabble-rousing actions like cooking sausage during Lent.

Suggested Core Texts
The Augsburg Confession, Articles XV, XXVI
The Tetrapolitan Confession, Chapters VII, VIII, IX
The Confutatio Pontificia, Defense to Articles XV, XXVI
Zwingli, *Of the Clarity and Certainty of the Word of God*
Eck, *Enchiridion of Commonplaces and Articles on the New Teachings*, Chapter 14
Melanchthon, *Apology of the Augsburg Confession*, Articles IX, XV

Scriptural Sources
New Testament: Matthew 4:1–4; Luke 5:33–35; 1 Timothy 4:1–4; 1 Corinthians 8:8–13; Colossians 2:16; James 2:14–26

Additional Sources
Zwingli, *Freedom of Choice in the Selection of Food*, in G. R. Potter, ed., *Huldrych Zwingli* (New York: St. Martin's Press, 1977) 17–18.

Issue 3: Baptism and Original Sin: What Should Be Done about the Anabaptists?

Reformers are united in recognizing baptism, along with the Eucharist, as the two traditional sacraments with a basis in scripture. Unlike the Eucharist, most reformers differ only slightly from traditionalists in their understanding of the meaning and performance of baptism. However, some more radical reformers have concluded that baptism should be performed only for adults, since the Bible includes no stories of infants or children being baptized. Those holding this view are known as Anabaptists, or Re-baptizers (*Wiedertäufer*), since they reject their infant baptism and undergo a second, adult baptism when they choose to join the Anabaptist community. Christians have traditionally baptized infants to remove original sin—the state of sinfulness that adheres to all descendants of Adam and Eve, the first humans who disobeyed God in the Garden of Eden. If an unbaptized infant were to die, as many infants did, the stain of original sin means they could not be buried in a Christian cemetery and their souls could never go to heaven. The rejection of infant baptism is extremely significant, then, because refusal to baptize a child would consign that child to **limbo**, a place between heaven and hell where the soul could never escape. And this is just one of many beliefs that make Anabaptists potentially dangerous: they consider themselves separate from the rest of the Christian community, refuse to serve as magistrates, are strict pacifists even when it comes to town defense, and refuse to swear oaths. What should be done to deter the spread of Anabaptism in Augsburg—and what should be done with Anabaptists caught by authorities?

Suggested Core Texts
The Augsburg Confession, Article IX
The Tetrapolitan Confession, Chapter XVII
The Confutatio Pontificia, Defense to Article IX
The Schleitheim Confession
Luther, *Small Catechism*
Melanchthon, *Apology of the Augsburg Confession*, Article IX
Interrogations of Suspected Anabaptists

Scriptural Sources
New Testament: Mark 1:2–11; Mark 16:15–16; 1 Corinthians 12:12–14; Colossians 2:8–17

Issue 4: Art and Iconoclasm: What Should Be Done about the Paintings, Statues, Stained Glass, and Other Ornate Furnishings in the Churches?

Augsburg's wealth is reflected in the gorgeous decoration of its churches. Many families, even those of relatively modest means, have donated altar images, stained glass windows, rich textiles and carpets, and sacred vessels of gold and silver for use in the performance of the Eucharist. Some reformers want to clear the churches of these objects so parishioners' attention can be focused entirely on the Word of God. Other reformers only want to get rid of problematic pieces, such as statues or paintings of saints that might be worshipped by an ignorant populace. But discussion of art and decoration is fraught: people grow attached to their favorite pieces, and traditionalists argue that art inclines the mind toward God. Surely these magnificent objects should not be destroyed!

It is impossible to overestimate the significance of religious art to the people of Augsburg. For the poor, the church is the only place they can go to see beautiful objects that could provide a vision of what heaven might be like. The illiterate—which is almost everyone—rely on paintings and sculpture to teach them the stories of the Bible and church history. For wealthier families, the donation of art and placement of family memorials in the churches signifies a visual representation of their place within Augsburg's social hierarchy: the objects they donate are often extraordinarily valuable. The artist and goldsmith guilds in Augsburg rely on commissions of religious art for a significant portion of their work. And it is not only Augsburgers who donate art to churches: the Cathedral of Our Lady and Basilica of Sts. Ulrich and Afra contain many valuable pieces given by noble lords from Bavaria and elsewhere. Any discussion of art in Augsburg's churches must consider the political, social, and financial implications of removing images.

Suggested Core Texts

The Augsburg Confession, Article XXI
The Tetrapolitan Confession, Chapter XXII
The Confutatio Pontificia, Defense to Article XXI
Eck, *Enchiridion of Commonplaces and Articles on the New Teachings*, Chapter 16
Luther, *Against the Heavenly Prophets in the Matter of Images and Sacraments*

Scriptural Sources

Old Testament: Exodus 20:4; Deuteronomy 4:15–19; Deuteronomy 7:4–6

Issue 5: The Sacraments: How Should Augsburg's Churches Celebrate the Eucharist?

The question of how the Eucharist should be observed is the most hotly contested Reformation issue—and arguably the most significant. Christian tradition holds that the wine and the wafer of bread become the true blood and body of God, in the person of Jesus Christ, when consecrated in Latin by a priest. This change, known as **transubstantiation**, affects the essence of the wine and bread, but not the outward appearance, which remains unchanged. Reformers wish to retain the observation of the Eucharist as one of two holy sacraments that are found in the Bible. But reformers do not agree on what the Eucharist means. When scripture says "This is my body," does it mean that the literal body of God is present? If so, how and where? When scripture says "Do this in remembrance of me," does it mean that the whole ritual is symbolic rather than literal? (See Luke 22:19.)

The followers of the traditional Roman church make sense of the mystery of transubstantiation by reference to Aristotelian physics. Aristotle wrote that all things have both a true essence ("substance") and a physical appearance ("accident"). The prayer of the priest transforms the substance—or essence—of the bread and wine into the body and blood of Christ, while the accident—or appearance—remains unchanged. This is how a consecrated wafer can look and taste like bread even though it has changed into the body of Christ. Luther rejects the concept of transubstantiation, with its Aristotelian dichotomy of substance and accident. But he holds on to a belief that the bread and wine become infused with a distillation of Christ's physical presence, so the elements of the Eucharist are really bread and wine at the same time as they are really Christ's body and blood. The "real presence" of Christ is there, not displacing the essence of the bread and wine, but existing alongside and through it. (Theologians sometimes refer to Luther's view as "consubstantiation.") Zwingli and his followers mostly reject belief in the physical presence of Christ in the elements of the Eucharist. But they allow that Christ must be spiritually present somehow and somewhere in the bread and wine, or perhaps Christ's presence is just there in the room among the congregation involved in the ritual. After all, the scriptures clearly say "This is my body," and the Swiss reformers take scripture seriously.

Tied up in these discussions about the meaning of the Eucharist elements is the issue of how regular people can and should participate. Traditionally, people have been allowed to observe the Latin consecration prayers and are subsequently offered the consecrated wafer of bread to consume, while priests consume the consecrated wine on behalf of the congregation. But some reformers are demanding that people be given an opportunity for communion "in both kinds"—that is, a chance to take the wine as well as the wafer. Is this really necessary? And reformers are calling for the consecration prayers to be said in German so all can understand them. But would a transition from the special, holy church language of Latin diminish the profound mystery of Christ's presence?

Augsburg's city council must decide on three issues related to the practice of the Eucharist: (1) whether the body of Christ is truly present in the bread and wine; (2) whether common laypeople should be offered the wine as well as the wafer of bread; and (3) whether the consecrating prayers should take place in Latin or German. If the city council of Augsburg can resolve these three issues, then it can establish a unified practice of the sacrament throughout Augsburg's churches and finally put the controversy over the Eucharist to rest.

Suggested Core Texts

The Augsburg Confession, Articles X, XIII, XXII
The Tetrapolitan Confession, Chapters XVI, XVIII,
The Confutatio Pontificia, Defense to Articles X, XIII, XXII
Eck, *Enchiridion of Commonplaces and Articles on the New Teachings*, Chapters 10, 37
Luther, *Small Catechism*
Melanchthon, *Apology of the Augsburg Confession*, Articles X, XXI, XXII

Scriptural Sources

New Testament: Matthew 26:26–29; Mark 14:22–24; Luke 22:13–20; 1 Corinthians 10:16–17; and 11:22–29

Political and Military Alliances

Whatever position Augsburg takes on religious issues, the city is going to need friends. The Reformation has thrown the Holy Roman Empire into chaos, and ambitious dukes and princes are already looking to take advantage of the situation to expand their territories or advance their interests. Wealthy Augsburg is a tempting prize. The challenge will be to find allies that align with Augsburg's religious interests and have sufficient strength to deter potential enemies. Luckily, Augsburg has some options:

1. Resurrect the Swabian League

The Swabian League was established in 1488, and for decades it has operated as a strong and successful mutual-defense organization, uniting free imperial cities (like Augsburg and Nuremberg) with various territories controlled by knights, dukes, and archbishops in the southern part of the empire. Members of the Swabian League share financial responsibility for 12,000 mercenary infantry and 1,200 cavalry, which successfully put down the Knights' Revolt in 1523 and the Peasants' War of 1524–25. The league has also dissuaded Bavaria from taking over wealthy towns like Augsburg that are near its borders. But the league has always been closely associated with princes of the Habsburg family and prelates of the church in Rome, so reform-minded cities and territories began leaving the league in the 1520s as disagreements over the Reformation intensified.

The remaining members of the Swabian League are loyal to the Roman church but lack direction and strong leadership. If Augsburg were to stay faithful to the pope and endorse the *Confutatio Pontificia*, it could reconstitute the Swabian League with the support of Emperor Charles V and become a major player in imperial politics. In fact, council member Ulrich Arzt has served as a military officer with the Swabian League and is well prepared to take over the leadership of the league. Augsburg's wealth and good management of the league could attract new members, ensure the city's protection, and preserve its own status as the preeminent financial center of the southern empire.

2. Join the New Schmalkaldic League
Philip of Hesse and Johann Friedrich of Saxony, two of the most powerful dukes aligned with Wittenberg, recently met in the town of Schmalkalden to establish a new alliance. The new **Schmalkaldic League** will protect reforming cities and territories and guard their plans for reform against possible military intervention by Charles V and his Rome-oriented allies. The two dukes have recruited into the Schmalkaldic League a total of twenty-three cities and territories—a minority of the imperial states leaning toward reform, but still a significant number.

Leaders of the Schmalkaldic League have made it clear that Augsburg is welcome to join them. But there is a catch. The league is anxious to avoid conflict among its members, so they require that Martin Luther approve the reform plan for all new members. If Augsburg wants to join the Schmalkaldic League, the city must endorse the *Augsburg Confession*, or otherwise convince Martin Luther that the city's plans for reform are in line with the priorities of Wittenberg.

3. Create a New System of Alliances
Some reform-leaning cities and territories have balked at the Schmalkaldic League's insistence on Wittenberg-style reform for all members, but there currently is no other organized option for cities and territories that want to reform in their own way. Fortunately, Augsburg has a very good relationship with two nearby imperial cities: Nuremberg and Ulm. As long as Augsburg does not choose a religious order aligned with Rome, these cities are willing to join Augsburg in a **Three-Cities League,** and each will pledge 1,300 soldiers and 13,000 **gulden** to one another's defense. This is helpful, but not enough to dissuade Charles V or his allies in Bavaria from threatening Augsburg.

If Augsburg chooses Swiss-style reform or develops its own system, it will need to bolster the Three-Cities League with additional allies. Endorsing the *Tetrapolitan Confession* will guarantee the cooperation of the Tetrapolitan cities: Constance, Memmingen, Lindau, but especially Strasbourg, which is the largest and wealthiest of the bunch. If you can persuade Strasbourg to agree to an alliance with Augsburg, then you have the best chance of convincing other cities and territories to do the same. Leveraging personal contacts between the Rehlinger family and their Strasbourg cousin, the reformer **Jakob Sturm**, is the best way to make this happen in the absence of a clear endorsement of the *Tetrapolitan Confession*. Though it may not initially be as powerful as the other leagues, a Three-Cities alliance—together with Strasbourg—may at least serve as a deterrent against those who might want to force Augsburg to change its religious practices, or share its wealth, through military invasion.

Suggested Sources (Not Included in Core Texts)
Christopher Close, *The Negotiated Reformation: Imperial Cities and the Politics of Urban Reform, 1525–1550* (New York: Cambridge University Press, 2009), 29–36, 61–76.

Peter H. Wilson, *Heart of Europe: A History of the Holy Roman Empire* (Cambridge, MA: Belknap Press of Harvard University Press, 2016), 562–65.

Raising Taxes
Like all politicians everywhere, the members of Augsburg's city council must figure out how to pay for any new initiatives. So, if Augsburg wants to hire more professional soldiers for defense or buy food to feed the hungry (and make them less likely to revolt), the city council will have to raise new revenue.

The basic currency used in Augsburg is the gulden, or "gold coin." Two hundred *pfenig* (pennies) equal one gulden. Most tradesmen and craftsmen earn around one gulden per week, or fifty gulden per year. Unskilled day laborers earn less, while well-established tradesmen and those with investments

Gulden coin, minted in Augsburg, ca. 1560. Wikimedia Commons.

earn more. Professional soldiers earn around one and a half gulden per week, or seventy-five gulden per year. Important city officials like Conrad Peutinger earn as much as 200 gulden per year.

In 1530, all heads of households in Augsburg pay a "head tax" of thirty pfenig and a defense tax of six pfenig as well as .25 percent (one-quarter of one percent) of the value of fixed goods (houses, land, silver mines) and .5 percent (one-half of one percent) on movable goods (cash, merchandise, money on loan). With a population of 30,000, we can assume that there are approximately 5,000 taxpaying heads of households in Augsburg and the current yearly income to the city from taxes on fixed and movable property is 100,000 gulden. To increase tax revenue, the city council has several different options:

1. Raise the Head Tax or Defense Tax, or Both
Changes to the head tax or defense tax would affect everyone equally, but note that these taxes are highly regressive—that is, the wealthy pay a much lower proportion of their income toward these types of taxes than the poor do.

2. Call for a Tax Reassessment
The value of a person's goods was regularly reassessed every seven to ten years. With Augsburg's economy growing so fast, a tax reassessment would raise the taxes of citizens who have a significant level of wealth and almost certainly raise the taxes of those whose wealth is moderate but rising. Those whose fortunes are falling would pay lower taxes, and at the bottom of the wealth scale, taxes would probably remain unchanged. At the rate the city is growing economically, a tax reassessment would yield an additional 15 percent, or 15,000 gulden, enough to pay the salaries of 200 soldiers or fund poor relief for six months.

3. Raise the Excise Tax on Beer and Wine
Excise taxes account for about half of Augsburg's yearly tax income, or about 100,000 gulden. Taxes are only charged on beer or wine consumed in a "public house" or tavern; alcoholic beverages produced at home for household consumption are not taxed. Raising excise taxes is a good way to earn more revenue, but it is very unpopular with the common people. Recall that one of the demands of protestors during the Schilling Revolt of 1524 was the repeal of excise taxes on beer!

4. Close Excise Tax Loopholes
The Gentlemen's Drinking Club is considered a "home" for tax purposes, so beverage consumption there is not taxed. Church institutions are also exempt from excise taxes, even though monasteries make money selling the beer they brew. The council could raise additional revenue by ending these special tax privileges. But take care: the Roman church will see any attempt to tax beer production and sales by monasteries as a serious threat to its sovereignty, and members of the Gentlemen's Drinking Club will likely protest this violation of their traditional privileges. Each source would bring in 10,000 gulden per year.

Suggested Sources (Not Included in Core Texts)
B. Ann Tlusty, "Full Cups, Full Coffers: Tax Strategies and Consumer Culture in the Early Modern German Cities," *German History* 32, no. 1 (2014): 1–28.

A Note on Religious Toleration

You may be tempted to come to a solution that allows for the coexistence of different religions. *This should be an absolute last resort.* Keep in mind that your primary task is to foster communal unity. Maintaining a diversity of religions creates no end of social and political problems—as Augsburg has already discovered. Not to mention that you risk bringing down the wrath of God on the city for harboring heretical religious practices. It is a risk few other cities have been willing to take. If you find that, despite your best efforts, you have no other option but to recognize more than one religion, you must address the following challenges:

- Where will members of the minority religion worship? If they are granted a church or churches to use, which one(s)? And how will you compensate the majority religion for giving up a church to a minority group?
- How will the council control the minority clergy? Will the council pay their salary? What restrictions will be placed on their activity?
- What will the council do to ensure that religious diversity does not lead to conflict, particularly on religious holidays and during processions?
- Will members of the minority have the same rights as the majority?
- How will you explain to potential allies why groups opposed to the religious viewpoint of the league are allowed to remain in the city?

RULES AND PROCEDURES

As members of the city council of Augsburg, your primary tasks are to promote peace and unity within the city, settle conflicts, and protect the integrity of the city and its interests from assault from within or without. The challenge posed by the Reformation is your most serious test yet, one that will require you to balance various interests to achieve your goal of a prosperous, harmonious city. The danger is high that decisions made by the council could provoke another major urban uprising or cause Charles V to return to Augsburg and impose his will by force.

Leadership: The members of the council will elect two mayors: one guild master and one patrician. The elected mayors will be assisted by council clerk Peutinger. Those elected to the office of mayor are automatically welcomed into the Gentlemen's Drinking Club if they are not already a member.

Memoranda: The theological and political issues are complex, so the council frequently assigns one or more of its members to research a topic and present their findings to the council. Every member of the council should expect to be assigned one or more memoranda to research and present, or members may be assigned to write a response to the memoranda presented by others. Council members may also be assigned other tasks, such as writing letters or negotiating on behalf of the council. (See individual role descriptions for details.)

Procedures: In each council session, the mayors will call for the presentation of memoranda on a particular topic, after which discussion can take place. All members of the council should be careful to address each other with the decorum and formality that befits members of the Gentlemen's Drinking Club—or those who wish to become members. When the time comes for a decision to be made, proposals should be written clearly on the board for all to see.

Voting: Each member of the city council has one vote, with the exception of the council clerk. Peutinger votes only in the event of a tie. (In a small class, the GM may decide to give Peutinger a vote.)

Expenditures and Taxes: Some members of the council are fabulously wealthy, but nobody has much liquid capital. Wealth is tied up in goods or loans. Thus, *it is not possible for even the wealthiest council members to undertake poor relief or civic defense on their own.* Any increase to city expenditures must be offset by either a decrease in spending in some area or an increase in taxes. The council may choose to increase the head tax or defense tax paid by all inhabitants of the city, enact a tax reassessment to increase taxes on those whose businesses are thriving, increase excise taxes on beer and wine, or close tax loopholes. All of these choices—or combinations of them—come with potential consequences.

The Gentlemen's Drinking Club

Some high-status or wealthy councillors are members of the prestigious Gentlemen's Drinking Club. Members of the club—and *only* members—have access to the club rooms across the street from the council meeting house. An adjournment of the council can be called at any time with the agreement of at least two of the three council leaders (the two mayors and Peutinger). While relaxing together in the Drinking Club, members are welcome to discuss and decide on all kinds of issues without having to consult councillors from the lower orders. The instructor may opt to limit the length of the Drinking Club meetings. Nonmembers can observe but not participate in the meetings. The Gentlemen's Drinking Club can

- Hold discussions of the issues that exclude the voices of nonmembers.
- Overturn any decision of the city council by majority vote.
- Admit new members by majority vote. Once admitted, a member may not be dismissed except by unanimous vote.

Hiring Mercenary Soldiers

Most towns are defended by a town guard made up of trained male citizens ready to respond to threats at the tolling of a certain bell. However, by the sixteenth century, most major towns also employed professional mercenary soldiers. In 1530, the city council of Augsburg paid 600 mercenary soldiers to patrol the streets and discourage attack from without and rebellion from within. It is possible for the council to hire additional soldiers if it wishes, but it must find a way to reduce other expenses or increase tax revenue. The cost of one mercenary soldier is approximately six gulden per month, or seventy-five gulden per year.

Sentencing Criminals and Anabaptists

The city council is occasionally called upon to pass judgment on those convicted of serious crimes, including Anabaptism. Note that while prisoners can be temporarily confined in a gatehouse, long-term imprisonment is not an option in the sixteenth century. When convicted Anabaptists are brought before the council, they are generally given one of the following sentences:

- The prisoner is released without punishment.
- The prisoner is given an opportunity to recant their beliefs and publicly reject the *Schleitheim Confession*. If they do this, they are allowed to go free.
- The prisoner is exiled from Augsburg for a period of five years, with or without recanting their beliefs.
- The prisoner is exiled from Augsburg permanently, and all of their property is confiscated.
- The prisoner is beheaded with a sword, then burned at the stake.
- The prisoner is burned alive at the stake.

STANDARD GAME SCHEDULE

(Designed for seventy-five-minute class sessions. Your GM may institute a different schedule.)

Game Session 1
- Election of mayors: Peutinger leads the election. One mayor must be a guild master, one a patrician.
- Discussion of priestly marriage: presentation of memoranda. A more general discussion should follow, including less formal speeches by other members of the council. Negotiations can take place, but no final decision should be made until the following session.
- Discussion of Lent and the eating of sausages: presentation of memoranda, followed by discussion and negotiation.
- Introduction of Anabaptist testimony.

Game Session 2
- Discussion and decision on marriage of priests: an Indeterminate council member may be assigned to give a response. Likely others will also wish to say something. The council should then vote on what position Augsburg will take on priestly marriage—one vote per council member.
- Discussion and decision on Lent: an Indeterminate council member may be assigned to present a response, followed by final discussion and vote.
- Sentencing of the Anabaptists: several members of the council may be assigned to present formal positions on the sentencing of Anabaptists before a general discussion takes place. In a smaller class, a general discussion can suffice.
- Other issues may come up, including legislation to prevent Anabaptism, the problem of Bavarian trade, or proposed changes in taxes.

Game Session 3
- Response and discussion of any outstanding issues from previous session.
- Discussion of art and iconoclasm: presentation of memoranda, followed by discussion. No final decision should be made until next session.
- Discussion of the Eucharist: presentation of memoranda, followed by discussion. No final decision should be made until next session.
- Securing alliances and other issues may come up.

Game Session 4
- Response to any issues from previous session.
- Discussion and decision on art and iconoclasm: an Indeterminate council member may be assigned to present a response. Others may also have opinions to share. The council should make a decision regarding art in the churches.
- Discussion and decision on the Eucharist: an Indeterminate council member may be assigned to present a response. Others may speak. A decision may be made right away or rolled into the discussion of whether to endorse one of the formal confessions.
- Discussion and decision on alliances and the endorsement of a confession: in a larger class, several council members will present formal recommendations regarding alliances, which may or may not involve endorsing one of the three confessions. In a smaller class, everyone should be encouraged to speak on these issues. Council members may choose to endorse one of the confessions, they may modify it, or they may put together their own unique alternative. Either way, the council *must* come to a decision and *must* have a plan for self-defense by the end of this session.

Game Session 5: Postmortem
- Conrad Peutinger will present his letter to Emperor Charles V, explaining the decisions made by the council, and most likely urge him not to invade.
- George Vetter will present his letter to the people of Augsburg, explaining the decisions made by the council and urging them not to revolt.
- The instructor will roll a die to determine the final outcome. The die rolls may be modified by how strong one or both speeches are, as well as by the decisions made over the course of the city council's deliberations.
- The game is now over. The instructor will use the remainder of the time as an open discussion with the students about what they learned and will explain what happened historically during the Reformation in Augsburg.

4

Roles and Factions

ROMAN FACTION

The Roman church has existed as the dominant spiritual and political institution in western Europe for more than a thousand years. The church needs some reform, to be sure. But there is no need to throw out centuries of tradition. Why trust the word of obscure monks and renegade priests against all the fathers of the church? Many believe that Augsburg's strongest way forward is to support the pope, resurrect the Swabian League, and endorse the *Confutatio Pontificia*.

Conrad Peutinger: The civic secretary to the city council of Augsburg and among the most well-educated and well-connected inhabitants of the city. Peutinger has represented Augsburg at numerous imperial diets and reichstags. He has a significant level of wealth, paying an estimated 100 gulden in taxes. He is a member of the Gentlemen's Drinking Club.

Ulrich Arzt: One of the guild masters of the Merchants' Guild and brother-in-law of Jakob Fugger, but his personal wealth is relatively modest and has diminished over time. He currently pays only twenty-two gulden in taxes. Arzt has served as an officer in the Swabian League and is a member of the Gentlemen's Drinking Club.

Franz Brigel: Guild master of the Butchers' Guild and relatively poor, compared to other council members, paying only two gulden in taxes. His business is dependent on meat from Bavaria.

Hans Rehlinger: A member of the patrician Rehlinger family and businessman, the father-in-law of Anton Fugger, a creditor to Charles V and a speculator in the international silver and mercury markets. He is only moderately wealthy, paying eighty-one gulden in taxes, but his fortunes are rising. He is a member of the Gentlemen's Drinking Club.

Mattheus Langenmantel: An up-and-coming young patrician with excellent connections, especially to the dukes of Bavaria. But he has no businesses or wealth of his own—yet. He pays an estimated thirty gulden in taxes and his fortunes are rising.

Ambrosius Höchstetter: Guild master of the Merchants' Guild. He has a rapidly expanding international business empire and significant wealth, paying 275 gulden in taxes. He is a member of the Gentlemen's Drinking Club.

Wilhelm Rehlinger: Patrician of modest but diminishing wealth with business interests in silks and spices. He pays thirty-four gulden in taxes. He has a degree from the University of Ingolstadt, which is unusual for the council. He is a member of the Gentlemen's Drinking Club.

WITTENBERG FACTION

For safety, Martin Luther has retreated to Wittenberg under the protection of the Duke of Saxony and a new alliance of princes and cities: the Schmalkaldic League. Priests and theologians like Philip Melanchthon who support Luther's vision of reform have likewise gathered in Wittenberg. There Luther and his colleagues train pastors and write treatises expounding on the kind of church reform that is desperately needed but relatively moderate, preserving the essential elements of Christian worship while removing centuries of unnecessary traditions, sentiments expressed in the *Augsburg Confession*. Followers of Wittenberg-style reform firmly believe that the church in Rome will eventually recognize the wisdom of church practices based in scripture and the value of strong partnerships between religious and secular powers.

George Vetter: Patrician, connected by marriage to the powerful Welser family, but of very modest means and a dwindling fortune. He pays twelve gulden in taxes. Personal friend to Martin Luther and correspondent of Ulrich Zwingli. Well trusted by the people of Augsburg.

Christoph Herwart: Very wealthy patrician of ancient family, engaged in moneylending and other international business ventures with the Fugger firms, Conrad Rehlinger, and Anton Haug. His wealth is significant, and he pays 223 gulden in taxes. He is a member of the Gentlemen's Drinking Club.

Hieronymus Imhof: A very wealthy guild master of the Merchants' Guild. He is close friends with Anton Fugger and frequently partners with the Fugger merchants in silver trade and moneylending. He pays 182 gulden in taxes. He is a member of the Gentlemen's Drinking Club.

Conrad Rehlinger: Very wealthy patrician with strong business connections to Venice and banking partnerships with the Fuggers and Christoph Herwart. He is a moneylender to kings including Ferdinand of Bohemia. His fortune is significant, paying 280 gulden in taxes. He is a member of the Gentlemen's Drinking Club.

Servatius Kohler: Guild master of the Wool Guild and deeply connected to the weaver communities that live in St. Jakob's quarter of Augsburg. He is a shop owner of little wealth, paying only five gulden in taxes.

Wolfgang Rehlinger: Young patrician employed by the firm of Ambrosius Höchstetter, cousin to Ulrich Rehlinger and closely related to the Strasbourg reformer Jakob Sturm. His fortunes are currently moderate—he pays only thirty gulden in taxes—but his business is expanding rapidly.

SWISS FACTION

Ulrich Zwingli emerged as a major voice for reform in the Swiss cantons and southern empire around the time Martin Luther began to gain followers in the north and east. Zwingli and other Swiss-style reformers espouse a more complete and thorough reform, breaking more firmly with church tradition than the Wittenberg reformers. The Swiss position is articulated in the *Tetrapolitan Confession* and the writings of Zwingli. The Swiss approach is popular in independent cities like Augsburg for its emphasis on communal values.

Anton Bimmel: Guild master of the Weavers' Guild, responsible for Augsburg's most important local industry, and also engaged with the Fugger firms and other international moneylending interests. He rose from a modest background to great wealth, currently paying 185 gulden in taxes. Bimmel is Zwingli's first and staunchest advocate in Augsburg.

Ulrich Rehlinger: Wealthy patrician, cousin of Wolfgang Rehlinger and close relative of Strasbourg reformer Jakob Sturm. Investment partner to Anton Fugger with rising fortunes; he currently pays 156 gulden in taxes. He corresponds with many reformers and openly attends priests' weddings. He is a member of the Gentlemen's Drinking Club.

Daniel Hopfer: Guild master of the Ironworkers' Guild, decorator of armor and creator of etched images for printed pamphlets. He was awarded a family crest by his favorite customer, Emperor Charles V. As a tradesman, he has a relatively low level of wealth, paying an estimated eight gulden in taxes.

Magnus Seitz: Guild master of the Weavers' Guild, working alongside Anton Bimmel but with only a small fraction of his wealth. He currently pays twelve gulden in taxes per year, but his fortunes are rising. Generations of his family have served as guild masters, forging deep connections throughout the community of weavers.

Hans Welser: Young patrician, relatively new to Augsburg, and son-in-law of Philip Adler. He is an up-and-coming banker with interests in the Spanish saffron trade and an already-significant amount of wealth, paying 100 gulden in taxes.

Paul Wittelspeck: Guild master of the Shopkeepers' Guild. Poorest of the city council members, but also the most representative of the interests of the city's commoners, whom he sees in his shop daily. He pays two gulden in taxes.

INDETERMINATES (NO ASSIGNED FACTION)

These are difficult issues to grapple with, and salvation is at stake. Not everyone was entirely sure how to approach reform, and many were open to persuasion about what approach the city council ought to take. But "Indeterminate" does not necessarily mean moderate or indecisive. These people may take very strong positions and align with one or more factions once they are persuaded to do so.

Philip Adler: Guild master of the Salt Guild. Wealthiest member of the city council due to a near-monopoly on the salt trade; he pays 500 gulden in taxes. He is a creditor to Charles V and other Habsburg royalty, a member of the imperial council, and a member of the Gentlemen's Drinking Club.

Simprecht Hoser: Guild master of the Salt Guild, relatively young but rising in wealth and importance. He pays fifty-five gulden in taxes. He is a debtor and depositor with the Fugger Bank and creditor to Anton Haug.

Stephan Eiselin: Guild master of the Shopkeepers' Guild, the third-largest guild in Augsburg. He is modestly wealthy, paying seventy-seven gulden in taxes, but he has a rising net worth.

Ulrich Hieber: Guild master of the Cloakmakers' Guild. Despite making sable and mink clothing for people of great status throughout Europe, he is among the poorest members of the city council, paying only two gulden in taxes.

Caspar Mair: Guild master of the Brewers' Guild. He is relatively poor, paying only two gulden in taxes, but his profession is essential to all citizens of Augsburg.

Jos Fenenberg: Guild master of the Grocers' Guild. He is not wealthy, but comfortable, paying eight gulden in taxes. Shop owner who has daily interactions with the normal folks of Augsburg.

Anton Haug: Guild master of the Salt Guild with a rapidly growing international business involving salt mining in Salzburg and moneylending. He has business connections to Christoph Herwart and is the employee and brother-in-law to Anton Bimmel. He pays 238 gulden in taxes.

Leo Ravensburger: Patrician, son-in-law of Christoph Herwart, and close friend of Conrad Peutinger. He traveled around the world as a representative of the Welser banking house, spending a few years on the island of Madeira. He has modest personal wealth, paying forty gulden in taxes. He is a member of the Gentlemen's Drinking Club.

Jörg Fürst: Guild master of the Bakers' Guild. He has little wealth and pays only two gulden in taxes.

5 Core Texts

MAIN TEXTS: THE THREE CONFESSIONS

The Augsburg Confession (1530), Selections

Martin Luther and his associates viewed with some suspicion Emperor Charles V's invitation to discuss religious reform at the 1530 Imperial Reichstag in Augsburg. Fearing for his safety, Luther stayed away from Augsburg and sent his close associate Philip Melanchthon to represent him. Melanchthon wrote a treatise for the emperor outlining what Luther and the Wittenberg reformers saw as the most important principles of the Christian faith (Articles I–XXI) and the most significant problems with the current Roman church (Articles XXII–XXVII). Melanchthon presented this to a group of sympathetic nobles on June 23, who indicated their support by signing the document. Then, two days later, German and Latin versions of this text were read aloud before the Reichstag assembly and presented to a disgruntled Charles V.

The Augsburg Confession *is the first official public statement of Martin Luther's vision of church reform. It outlines what supporters of Lutheran reform "confess"—that is, what they believe. For many decades afterward, followers of Luther indicated their religious affiliation by declaring themselves adherents to the Augsburg Confession. They did not widely describe themselves as "Lutheran" until the eighteenth century.*

In the text below, "we" (signers of the Augsburg Confession) offer the emperor a statement of what "they" (followers of Martin Luther) believe and teach. Philip Melanchthon presents a fuller discussion of many of these points in his "apology," or explanation, of the Augsburg Confession. *After the Diet of Augsburg, the pope issued a point-by-point refutation of the* Augsburg Confession *in the* Confutatio Pontificia. *Both texts are included in this book along with an alternative vision for religious reform, the* Tetrapolitan Confession.

Source: F. Bente, ed., *Triglot Concordia: The Symbolical Books of the Evangelical Lutheran Church: German-Latin-English* (St. Louis, MO: Concordia, 1921).

Preface

In obedience to Your Imperial Majesty's wishes, we offer, in this matter of religion, the Confession of our preachers and of ourselves, showing what manner of doctrine from the Holy Scriptures and the pure Word of God has been up to this time set forth in our lands, dukedoms, dominions, and cities, and taught in our churches.

Your Imperial Majesty, our most clement Lord, we are prepared to confer amicably concerning all possible ways and means, in order that we may come together, as far as this may be honorably done, and the matter between us on both sides being peacefully discussed without offensive strife, the dissension, by God's help, may be done away and brought back to one true accordant religion.

Article IX. Of Baptism

Of Baptism they teach that it is necessary to salvation, and that through Baptism is offered the grace of God, and that children are to be baptized who, being offered to God through Baptism are received into God's grace. They condemn the Anabaptists, who reject the baptism of children, and say that children are saved without Baptism.

Article X. Of the Lord's Supper

Of the Supper of the Lord they teach that the Body and Blood of Christ are truly present and are distributed to those who eat the Supper of the Lord; and they reject those that teach otherwise.

Article XIII. Of the Use of the Sacraments

Of the Use of the Sacraments, they teach that the Sacraments were ordained, not only to be marks of profession among men, but rather to be signs and testimonies of the will of God toward us, instituted to awaken and confirm faith in those who use them. Wherefore we must so use the Sacraments that faith be added to believe the promises which are offered and set forth through the Sacraments.

*[Lutheran reform reduces the number of recognized sacraments from seven to two: baptism and the **Lord's Supper**.]*

They therefore condemn those who teach that the Sacraments justify by the outward act, and who do not teach that, in the use of the Sacraments, faith which believes that sins are forgiven, is required.

Article XV: Of Ecclesiastical Usages (Traditions)

Of Usages in the church, they teach that those ought to be observed which may be observed without sin, and which are profitable unto tranquility and good order in the Church, as particular holy-days, festivals, and the like. Nevertheless, concerning such things men are admonished that consciences are not to be burdened, as though such observance was necessary to salvation.

They are admonished also that human traditions instituted to propitiate God, to merit grace, and to make satisfaction for sins, are opposed to the Gospel and the doctrine of faith. Wherefore vows and traditions concerning meats and days, etc., instituted to merit grace and to make satisfaction for sins, are useless and contrary to the Gospel.

Article XXI. Of the Worship of the Saints

Of the Worship of Saints they teach that the memory of saints may be set before us, that we may follow their faith and good works, according to our calling, as the Emperor may follow the example of David in making war to drive away the Turk from his country; for both are kings. But the Scripture teaches not the invocation of saints or to ask help of saints, since it sets before us the one Christ as the Mediator, Propitiation, High Priest, and Intercessor. He is to be prayed to, and has promised that He will hear our prayer; and this worship, He approves above all, to wit, that in all afflictions He be called upon, 1 John 2:1: "If any man sin, we have an Advocate with the Father," etc. This is about the Sum of our Doctrine, in which, as can be seen, there is nothing that varies from the Scriptures, or from the Church Catholic, or from the Church of Rome as known from its writers. This being the case, they judge harshly who insist that our teachers be regarded as **heretics**.

Article XXII: Of Both Kinds in the Sacrament

To the laity are given Both Kinds in the Sacrament of the Lord's Supper, because this usage has the commandment of the Lord in Matt. 26:27: "Drink ye all of it, where Christ has manifestly commanded concerning the cup that all should drink." *[By "both kinds," Melanchthon is referring to both the wine (blood) of Christ and the bread (body) of Christ. Traditionally, the bread was shared with regular people (the laity) but the wine was usually consumed only by priests.]*

And lest any man should craftily say that this refers only to priests, Paul in 1 Cor. 11:27 recites an example from which it appears that the whole congregation did use both kinds. And this usage has long remained in the Church, nor is it known when, or by whose authority, it was changed; although Cardinal Cusanus mentions the time when it was approved. Cyprian in some places testifies that the blood was given to the people. The same is testified by Jerome, who says, "The priests administer the Eucharist, and distribute the blood of Christ to the people." Only custom, not so ancient, has it otherwise. But it is evident that any custom introduced against the commandments of God is not to be allowed, as the Canons witness. But this custom has been received, not only against the Scripture, but also against the old Canons and the example of the Church. Therefore, if any preferred to use both kinds of the Sacrament, they ought not to have been compelled with offense to their consciences to do otherwise.

Article XXIII. Of the Marriage of Priests

There has been common complaint concerning the examples of priests who were not chaste. For that reason also Pope Pius is reported to have said that there were certain causes why marriage was taken away from priests, but that there were far weightier ones why it ought to be given back; for so Platina writes. Since, therefore, our priests were desirous to avoid these open scandals, they married wives, and taught that it was lawful for them to contract matrimony. First, because Paul says, 1 Cor. 7:2–9: "To avoid fornication, let every man have his own wife." Also: "It is better to marry than to burn." Secondly, Christ says, Matt. 19:11: "All men cannot receive this saying," where He teaches that not all men are fit to lead a single life; for God created man for procreation, Gen. 1:28. Nor is it in man's power, without a singular gift and work of God, to alter this creation. For it is manifest, and many have confessed that no good, honest, chaste life, no Christian, sincere, upright conduct has resulted (from the attempt), but a horrible, fearful unrest and torment of conscience has been felt by many until the end.

Therefore, those who are not fit to lead a single life ought to contract matrimony. For no man's law, no vow, can annul the commandment and ordinance of God. For these reasons the priests teach that it is lawful for them to marry wives. It is also evident that in the ancient church priests were married men. For Paul says, 1 Tim. 3:2, that a bishop should be chosen who is the husband of one wife. . . . Moreover, many God-fearing and intelligent people in high station are known frequently to have expressed misgivings that such enforced celibacy and depriving men of marriage (which God Himself has instituted and left free to men) has never produced any good results but has brought on many great and evil vices and much iniquity. Seeing also that, as the world is aging, man's nature is gradually growing weaker, it is well to guard that no more vices steal into Germany.

Furthermore, God ordained marriage to be a help against human infirmity. The Canons themselves say that the old rigor ought now and then, in the latter times, to be relaxed because of the weakness of men, which it is to be wished were done also in this matter. And it is to be expected that the churches shall at some time lack pastors if marriage is any longer forbidden.

But while the commandment of God is in force, while the custom of the Church is well known, while impure celibacy causes many scandals, adulteries, and other crimes deserving the punishments of just magistrates, yet it is a marvelous thing that in nothing is more cruelty exercised than against the marriage of priests. God has given commandment to honor marriage. By the laws of all well-ordered commonwealths, even among the heathen, marriage is most highly honored. But now men, and that, priests, are cruelly put to death, contrary to the intent of the Canons, for no other cause than marriage. Paul, in 1 Tim. 4:3, calls that a doctrine of devils which forbids marriage. This may now be readily understood when the law against marriage is maintained by such penalties.

Article XXVI. Of the Distinction of Meats

It has been the general persuasion, not of the people alone, but also of those teaching in the churches, that making Distinctions of Meats, and like traditions of men, are works profitable to merit grace, and able to make satisfactions for sins. And that the world so thought, appears from this, that new ceremonies, new orders, new holy-days, and new fastings were daily instituted, and the teachers in the churches did exact these works as a service necessary to merit grace, and did greatly terrify men's consciences, if they should omit any of these things. From this persuasion concerning traditions much detriment has resulted in the Church. *[Recall that Luther rejected the idea that "works"—good things individuals did to demonstrate their faith—could have any effect on their salvation. Luther believed that nobody deserved "grace" and that it could only be freely given by God, not earned through human actions.]*

First, the doctrine of grace and of the righteousness of faith has been obscured by it, which is the chief part of the Gospel, and ought to stand out as the most prominent in the Church, in order that the merit of Christ may be well known, and faith, which believes that sins are forgiven for Christ's sake be exalted far above works. Wherefore Paul also lays the greatest stress on this article, putting aside the Law and human traditions, in order to show that Christian righteousness is something else than such works, to wit, the faith which believes that sins are freely forgiven for Christ's sake. But this doctrine of Paul has been almost wholly smothered by traditions, which have produced an opinion that, by making distinctions in meats and like services, we must merit grace and righteousness.

Secondly, these traditions have obscured the commandments of God, because traditions were placed far above the commandments of God. Christianity was thought to consist wholly in the observance of certain holy-days, rites, fasts, and vestures. These observances had won for themselves the exalted title of being the spiritual life and the perfect life. Meanwhile the commandments of God, according to each one's calling, were without honor namely, that the father brought up his offspring, that the mother bore children, that the prince governed the commonwealth, —these were accounted works that were worldly and imperfect, and far below those glittering observances. And this error greatly tormented devout consciences, which grieved that they were held in an imperfect state of life, as in marriage, in the office of magistrate; or in other civil ministrations; on the other hand, they admired the monks and such like, and falsely imagined that the observances of such men were more acceptable to God. *[Arguments against the complex traditions around fasting in the church could also apply to other church traditions, such as priestly celibacy.]*

Thus, therefore, they have taught that by the observance of human traditions we cannot merit grace or be justified, and hence we must not think such observances necessary acts of worship. They add hereunto testimonies of Scripture. Christ, Matt. 15:3, defends the Apostles who had not observed the usual tradition, which, however, evidently pertains to a matter not unlawful, but indifferent, and to have a certain affinity with the purifications of the Law, and says, Matt. 15:9: "In vain do they worship Me with the commandments of men." He, therefore, does not exact an unprofitable service. Shortly after He adds, "Not that which goeth into the mouth defileth a man." So also Paul, Rom. 14:17, "The kingdom of God is not meat and drink." Col. 2:16: "Let no man, therefore, judge you in meat, or in drink, or in respect of an holy-day, or of the Sabbath-day." Also: "If ye be dead with Christ from the rudiments of the world, why, as though living in the world, are ye subject to ordinances: Touch not, taste not, handle not!" And Peter says, Acts 15:10, "Why tempt ye God to put a yoke upon the neck of the disciples, which neither our fathers nor we were able to bear? But we believe that through the grace of the Lord Jesus Christ we shall be saved, even as they." Here Peter forbids to burden the consciences with many rites, either of Moses or of others. And in 1 Tim. 4:1-3, Paul calls the prohibition of meats a doctrine of devils; for it is against the Gospel to institute or to do such works that by them we may merit grace, or as though Christianity could not exist without such service of God. Here our adversaries object that our teachers are opposed to discipline and mortification of the flesh, as Jovinian. But the contrary may be learned from the writings of our teachers. For they have always taught concerning the cross that it behooves Christians to bear afflictions. This is the true, earnest, and unfeigned mortification, to wit, to be exercised with diverse afflictions, and to be crucified with Christ.

Moreover, they teach that every Christian ought to train and subdue himself with bodily restraints, or bodily exercises and labors that neither satiety nor slothfulness tempt him to sin, but not that we may merit grace or make satisfaction for sins by such exercises. And such external discipline ought to be urged at all times, not only on a few and set days. So Christ commands, Luke 21:34, "Take heed lest your hearts be overcharged with surfeiting." Also Matt. 17:21, "This kind goeth not out but by prayer and fasting." Paul also says, 1 Cor. 9:27, "I keep under my body and bring it into subjection." Here he clearly shows that he was keeping under his body, not to merit forgiveness of sins by that discipline, but to have his body in subjection and fitted for spiritual things, and for the discharge of duty according to his calling. Therefore, we do not condemn fasting in itself, but the traditions which prescribe certain days and certain meats, with peril of conscience, as though such works were a necessary service.

Nevertheless, very many traditions are kept on our part, which conduce to good order in the Church, as the Order of Lessons in the Mass and the chief holy days. But, at the same time, men are warned that such observances do not justify before God, and that in such things it should not be made sin if they be omitted without offense.

Conclusion

These are the chief articles which seem to be in controversy. For although we might have spoken of more abuses, yet, to avoid undue length, we have set forth the chief points, from which the rest may be readily judged. There have been great complaints concerning indulgences, pilgrimages, and the abuse of excommunications. The parishes have been vexed in many ways by the dealers in indulgences. There were endless contentions between the pastors and the monks concerning the parochial right, confessions, burials, sermons on extraordinary occasions, and innumerable other things. Issues of this sort we have passed over so that the chief points in this matter, having been briefly set forth, might be the more readily understood. Nor has anything been here said or adduced to the reproach of anyone. Only those things have been recounted whereof we thought that it was necessary to speak, in order that it might be understood that in doctrine and ceremonies nothing has been received on our part against Scripture or the Church Catholic. For it is manifest that we have taken most diligent care that no new and ungodly doctrine should creep into our churches.

The above articles we desire to present in accordance with the edict of Your Imperial Majesty, in order to exhibit our Confession and let men see a summary of the doctrine of our teachers. If there is anything that anyone might desire in this Confession, we are ready, God willing, to present ampler information according to the Scriptures.

Your Imperial Majesty's faithful subjects:
John, Duke of Saxony, Elector.
George, Margrave of Brandenburg.
Ernest, Duke of Lueneberg.
Philip, Landgrave of Hesse.
John Frederick, Duke of Saxony.
Francis, Duke of Lueneburg.
Wolfgang, Prince of Anhalt.
Senate and Magistracy of Nuremburg.
Senate of Reutlingen.

The Tetrapolitan Confession (1530), Selections

Not all those who attended the Diet of Augsburg shared the same vision of religious reform. Martin Bucer presented Emperor Charles V with an alternate statement of reformed belief, signed by representatives of the cities of Strasbourg, Constance, Memmingen, and Lindau. The Tetrapolitan Confession *was heavily influenced by the ideas of the Swiss reformer Ulrich Zwingli. It is like the* Augsburg Confession *in some ways, but it places emphasis on different areas and presents a distinctive take on the reform of traditions and sacraments in the church. The* Tetrapolitan Confession *centers scriptural precedent and rejects canon law more forcefully than the* Augsburg Confession *does.*

Bucer and his coauthors wrote the Tetrapolitan Confession *partly to stake their religious claims before the emperor, but mostly to bring theological unity to those who supported a Swiss vision of reform. Bucer spent his lifetime trying to bring various reformers from Swiss and Wittenberg camps into agreement on a cohesive model of church reform; he failed. Even though some of the arguments and theological positions laid out in the* Tetrapolitan Confession *appear similar to those in the* Augsburg Confession, *the deep distrust and enmity between Martin Luther and Ulrich Zwingli meant that they and their followers refused to negotiate or compromise their positions.*

Source: Henry E. Jacobs, ed., *The Book of Concord: or The Symbolical Books of the Evangelical Lutheran Church* (Philadelphia: G. W. Frederick, 1888).

Exordium

Thy Worshipful Majesty, Most Powerful and Most Clement Emperor, hath commanded that the orders and estates of the Holy Empire, so far as concerns each and each hopes to act towards tranquillizing the Church, should present to him their opinion, reduced to writing in both languages, Latin and German, concerning religion, as well as concerning the errors and vices which have insinuated themselves in opposition thereto, for discussion and examination, to the end that thereby a mode and way may be found to restore to its place the pure doctrine, all errors being abolished.

We desire, as is right, to obey this command, which has not so much originated from a religious design that has in view the profit of the Church as it exhibits and savors of the unparalleled clemency and kindness whereby Thy Worshipful Majesty hath rendered himself so beloved by the entire world. For in these matters we have never sought anything else than that, those things being abrogated which are contrary to the holy Gospels and to Christ s commands, it may be allowed not only us, but also all others who have professed Christ to follow after his pure doctrine, which alone is vivifying. Wherefore we pray and most humbly beseech Thy Worshipful Majesty to be so disposed to us as to deign to hear and consider what we will present as a reason for the hope that is in us, in order that concerning these matters there may be no doubt that it has been above all our desire to aim only at that whereby we may please, first of all, our Creator and Restorer Christ, and afterward also Thy Worshipful Majesty.

Chapter VII. Of Prayers and Fasts

We have prayers and fasts, actions nevertheless the most holy and such as are especially proper for Christians, to which our ecclesiastics most diligently exhort their hearers. For true fasting is, as it were, a renouncing of the present life. Which is always subject to evil desires, and a meditation upon the future life that is free from perturbations. Prayer is a lifting up of the mind to God, and such conversation with him that no other thing so greatly inflames man with heavenly affections and more mightily conforms the mind to God's will. But however holy and necessary that exercises be to Christians, yet as one's neighbor is not so much served by them as man is prepared to serve his neighbor with profit, they are not to be preferred to holy doctrine, godly exhortations and admonitions, and other duties whereby our neighbor at once receives profit. Hence we read of the Savior that in the nighttime he gave himself to prayer, but in the daytime to doctrine and healing the sick. For as love is greater than faith and hope, so we believe that those things which come nearest—viz. such as bring assured profit unto men—are to be preferred above all other holy functions. Hence St. Chrysostom wrote that in the whole company of virtues fasting had the last place.

Chapter VIII. Of the Commanding of Fasts

But since no minds, unless they be very ardent and peculiarly influenced by inspiration from above, can either pray or fast aright and with profit, we believe that it is better, according to the example of the apostles and of the earlier and purer Church, by holy exhortations to invite men to these things, rather than to exhort them by precepts, especially such as bind men under penalty of sin, as the priests that have been of late, since the order of priests had not a little degenerated, undertook to do. So we prefer to leave the place, time and manner both of praying and of fasting to be determined by the Holy Ghost, without whom it is impossible for anyone either to pray or to fast aright, rather than prescribe them by fixed laws, especially such as may not be broken without some atonement.

When, therefore, we saw very evidently that the chief men in the Church beyond the authority of Scripture assumed this authority so to enjoin fasts as to bind men's consciences, we allowed consciences to be freed from these snares, but by the Scriptures, and especially Paul's writings, which with singular earnestness remove these rudiments of the world from the necks of Christians. For the saying of Paul ought not to have light weight with us: "Let no man, therefore, judge you in meat, or in drink, or in respect of a holy day, or of the new moon, or of the Sabbath days." And again: "Wherefore if ye be dead with Christ from the rudiments of the world, why, as though living in the world, are ye subject to ordinances?" For if St. Paul (than whom no man at any time taught Christ more certainly) maintains that through Christ we have obtained such liberty in external things that he not only allows no creature the right to burden those who believe in Christ, even with those ceremonies and observances which God himself appointed, and wished in their own time to be profitable, but also denounces as having fallen away from Christ, and that Christ is of none effect to those who suffer themselves to be made servant thereto, what verdict do we think should be passed on those commandments which men have devised of themselves, not only without any oracle, but also without any example worthy of being followed, and which, therefore, are unto most not only beggarly and weak, but also hurtful; not elements—i.e. rudiments of holy discipline—but impediments of true godliness? How much more unjust will it be for anyone to assume to himself this power over the inheritance of Christ, so as to oppress it with such bondage, and how far shall it remove us from Christ if we submit ourselves to these things!

Chapter IX. Of the Choice of Meats

For the same cause was remitted also the selection of meats prescribed for certain days, which St. Paul, writing to Timothy, calls a doctrine of demons. Nor is their answer firmly grounded who maintain that these expressions were used only against the Manicheans, Encratites, Tatianites and Marcionites, who wholly forbad certain kinds of meats and marriage. The apostle in this place condemned those who command "to abstain from meats which God hath created to be received," etc. Now they also who forbid the taking of certain meats on certain days nevertheless command men to abstain from meats which God created to be taken, and are akin to the doctrines of demons, as is manifest from the reason that the apostle added. For he says God has created everything that is good, and nothing is to be refused that is received with thanksgiving. He excepts no times, although no one favored frugality, temperance, and also choice chastisements of the flesh and lawful fastings, more than he did. Certainly, a Christian must observe frugality, but at all times; and the flesh must sometimes be chastised by diminishing the accustomed diet, but plainness and moderation of meats conduce to this more than does the kind. To conclude: it is meet for Christians now and then to take upon themselves a due fast; but that must not be an abstinence from certain but from all meats; nor from meats only, but from all the dainties whatsoever of this life. For what kind of fast is this, what sort of abstinence, to change only the kind of dainties (as those who are regarded today more devout than others are wont to do) unless, together with abstinence from meats, we are continent also from those things that are hurtful, and bestow much leisure upon the pursuit of spiritual things? *[Note the association here between fasting and marriage. Arguments against church traditions around fasting could also apply to the tradition of priestly celibacy.]*

Chapter XVI. Of the Sacraments
Furthermore, since the Church lives here in the flesh, even though not according to the flesh, it has pleased the Lord to teach, admonish and exhort it also by the outward Word; and that this might be done the more conveniently he wished his people to maintain an external society among themselves. For this reason he has also given to them sacred symbols, which we call sacraments. Among these, Baptism and the Lord's Supper are the chief. These we believe were called sacraments by the ancients, not only because they are visible signs of invisible grace (to use the words of St. Augustine), but also because in them a profession of faith, as it were, is made.

Chapter XVII. Of Baptism
Of Baptism, therefore, we confess that which Scripture in various places declares of it: that by it we are buried into Christ's death, are united into one body and put on Christ; that it is the washing of regeneration, that it washes away sins and saves us. All this we understand as St. Peter has interpreted when he says: "The like figure whereunto even baptism doth also now save us, not the putting away of the filth of the flesh, but the answer of a good conscience toward God." For without faith it is impossible to please God, and we are saved by grace, not by our works. But since Baptism is the sacrament of the covenant that God makes with those who are his, promising to be their God and Protector, as well as of their seed, and to have them as his people, and finally, since it is a symbol of renewing through the Spirit, which occurs through Christ, our theologians teach that it is to be given infants also, no less than formerly under Moses they were circumcised. For we are indeed the children of Abraham. Therefore no less to us than to those of old pertains the promise: I will be thy God and the God of thy seed.

[Compare St. Peter's statement to the Augsburg Confession*: the Tetrapolitan take on baptism is much more about symbolically joining a community of believers than it is about removing original sin.]*

Chapter XVIII. Of the Eucharist
Concerning this venerable sacrament of the body and blood of Christ, all that the evangelists, Paul and the holy fathers, have left in writing, our men, in the best faith, teach, commend and inculcate. And hence with singular zeal they always publish this goodness of Christ to his people, whereby no less today than at that last Supper, to all those who sincerely have given their names among his disciples and receive this Supper according to his institution, he deigns to give his true body and true blood to be truly eaten and drunk for the food and drink of souls, for their nourishment unto life eternal, so that now he may live and abide in them, and they in him, to be raised up by him at the last day to new and immortal life, according to his words of eternal truth: "Take, eat; this is my body," etc.; "drink ye all of it; for this is my blood," etc.

Now, our ecclesiastics with especial diligence withdraw the minds of our people both from all contention and from all superfluous and curious inquiry to that which is alone profitable, and which was alone regarded by Christ our Savior—namely, that, fed upon him, we may live in and through him a life pleasing to God, holy, and therefore eternal and blessed, and that we who partake of one bread in the Holy Supper may be among ourselves one bread and one body. Hence indeed it occurs that the divine sacraments, the Most Holy Supper of Christ, are administered and received among us very religiously and with singular reverence.

From these things, which are truly in this manner, Thy Most Worshipful Majesty, Most Clement Emperor, doth know how falsely our adversaries proclaim that our men change Christ's words and do them violence by human glosses; that nothing save mere bread and mere wine is administered in our Supper; and thus that among us the Lord's Supper has been despised and rejected. For with the greatest earnestness our men always teach and exhort that every man with simple faith embrace these words of the Lord, rejecting all devices and false glosses of men, and removing all wavering, apply his mind to their true meaning, and finally, with as great devotion as possible, receive these sacraments for the quickening nourishment of their souls and the grateful remembrance of so great a benefit; as is generally done now among us more frequently and devoutly than heretofore. Moreover, our ecclesiastics have always hitherto offered themselves, as they do today also, with all modesty and truth, in order to render an account of their faith and doctrine concerning all that they believe and teach touching this sacrament, as well as other things; and that not only to Thy Worshipful Majesty, but also to everyone who demands it.

Chapter XXII. Of Statues and Images

Finally, against statues and images our preachers have applied the holy oracles, chiefly because they began to be worshipped and adored openly, and vain expenditure was devoted to them that was due the hungry, thirsty and naked Christ; and lastly, because by their worship and the expenditure they required (both conflicting with God's word) they seek merits with God. Against this religious error they have interposed also the authority of the ancient Church, which undoubtedly abominated the sight of any image, whether painted or graven, in the church, as the deed of Epiphanius, bishop of Salamis in Cyprus, that he reports of himself, abundantly proves. For when he saw on a curtain in a certain church a painting of Christ or some saint (for he writes that he does not exactly remember), he was inflamed with such indignation because he saw an image of a man hanging in the church, contrary to the authority of the Scriptures and to our faith and religion, that he at once tore the curtain and ordered that the corpse of a poor man be wrapped therein.

For the declaration that is commonly made that by statues and images the more rude are taught and instructed will not suffice to prove that they should be carried, especially where they are adored by the populace. God's ancient people were of a ruder class, so that it was needful to instruct them by numerous ceremonies; nevertheless, God did not think that images were of such value to teach and instruct the more rude, since he forbad them among the very chief things. If the answer be made that God forbad such images as were worshipped, it immediately follows that when all have begun to adore them they should be universally removed from the churches, on account of the offence which they occasion. For all things in the Church should be directed to edification, much less should anything be tolerated which may give occasion for ruin and can contribute no advantage.

Our men also confess that in itself the use of images is free, but, free as it may be, the Christian must consider what is expedient, what edifies, and should use images in such place and manner as not to present a stumbling block to any. For Paul was prepared to have both meat and wine prohibited him for his entire life if he knew that either in any way injured the welfare of others.

Conclusion

These are the chief points, most invincible and devout Emperor, wherein our men have somewhat receded from the common doctrine of ecclesiastics, being forced thereto by the authority alone of the Scriptures, which is justly to be preferred above all other traditions. . . . These things, Most Godly Emperor, we here mention for no other reason than to show our obedience to thy wish that we should explain our opinion concerning the reformation of religion. For otherwise we have good hope that Thy Worshipful Majesty hast well considered and sees sufficiently what necessity urges us thereto, what fruit it invites, and finally how worthy a thing this is for Thy Worshipful Majesty, who is so much praised for religion and clemency, that, all the men in highest reputation for learning and godliness being assembled, the effort be made to learn what should be thought of each doctrine just now controverted, and then an explanation be made by suitable ministers of Christ, with all meekness and fidelity, to those who are believed to be detained in errors. The King of kings, Jesus Christ, grant Thy Worshipful Majesty in this matter, as well as in others, to do all things for his glory, and long preserve and happily advance thee in both health and prosperity, to the welfare of the entire Christian government! Amen.

The Confutatio Pontificia (1530), Selections

Confutatio Pontificia *is Latin for "The Pope's Response." This point-by-point reaction to the* Augsburg Confession *is also known as the* Confutatio Augustana, *or* Refutation of Augsburg. *It was written not by the pope personally but by a group of theologians, principally Martin Luther's old adversary Johann Maier von Eck. It was read at the Augsburg Reichstag on August 3, about six weeks after the* Augsburg Confession *was presented. By that point, of course, it was too late to engage the reformers in debate because the religious discussions at the Reichstag had already gone off the rails.*

It would take the Roman church until 1561 to finally agree on clear statements of Catholic doctrine and practice at the Council of Trent. But the Confutatio *stands as an interim declaration of where the Roman church stood on the major issues brought up by reformers. Its tone is conciliatory on most issues; the pope requested a statement that emphasized common ground as much as possible. Nevertheless, the* Confutatio *reinforces the significance of the doctrine of transubstantiation, the efficacy of "works" such as fasting and prayers to saints, the importance of priestly celibacy, and the dangers of disobedience to authority.*

Source: Henry E. Jacobs, ed., *The Book of Concord: or The Symbolical Books of the Evangelical Lutheran Church* (Philadelphia: G. W. Frederick, 1888).

Defense to Article IX [Baptism]

The ninth article, concerning Baptism—viz. that it is necessary to salvation, and that children ought to be baptized—is approved and accepted, and they are right in condemning the Anabaptists, a most seditious class of men that ought to be banished far from the boundaries of the Roman Empire in order that illustrious Germany may not suffer again such a destructive and sanguinary commotion as she experienced five years ago in the slaughter of so many thousands. *[The* Confutatio *conflates the Anabaptists with the peasants that rebelled in 1524–25.]*

Defense to Article X [The Lord's Supper]

The tenth article gives no offense in its words, because they confess that in the Eucharist, after the consecration lawfully made, the Body and Blood of Christ are substantially and truly present, if only they believe that the entire Christ is present under each form, so that the Blood of Christ is no less present under the form of bread by concomitance than it is under the form of the wine, and the reverse. Otherwise, in the Eucharist the Body of Christ is dead and bloodless, contrary to St. Paul, because "Christ, being raised from the dead, dieth no more," Rom. 6:9. One matter is added as very necessary to the article of the Confession—viz. that they believe the Church, rather than some teaching otherwise and incorrectly, that by the almighty Word of God in the consecration of the Eucharist the substance of the bread is changed into the Body of Christ. For thus in a general council it has been determined, canon Firmiter, concerning the exalted Trinity, and the Catholic faith. They are praised therefor, for condemning the Capernaites, who deny the truth of the Body and Blood of our Lord Jesus Christ in the Eucharist. *[The* Augsburg Confession *acknowledges that the body and blood of Christ are present in the Lord's Supper—but the* Confutatio *insists that Christ is fully present in both forms.]*

Defense to Article XIII [Sacraments]

The thirteenth article gives no offence, but is accepted, while they say that the sacraments were instituted not only to be marks of profession among men, but rather to be signs and testimonies of God's will toward us; nevertheless, we must request them that what they here ascribe to the sacraments in general they confess also specifically concerning the seven sacraments of the Church and take measures for the observance of them by their subjects.

Defense to Article XV [Ecclesiastical Usages / Church Traditions]

In the fifteenth article their confession that such **ecclesiastical** rites are to be observed as may be observed without sin, and are profitable for tranquility and good order in the church, is accepted, and they must be admonished that the princes and cities see to it that the ecclesiastical rites of the Church universal be observed in their dominions and districts, as well as those which have been kept devoutly and religiously in every province even to us, and if any of these have been intermitted that they restore them, and arrange, determine and effectually enjoin upon their subjects that all things be done in their churches according to the ancient form. Nevertheless, the appendix to this article must be entirely removed, since it is false that human ordinances instituted to propitiate God and make satisfactions for sins are opposed to the Gospel, as will be more amply declared hereafter concerning vows, the choice of food and the like.

Defense to Article XXI [Worship of the Saints]

In the last place, they present the twenty-first article, wherein they admit that the memory of saints may be set before us, that we may follow their faith and good works, but not that they be invoked and aid be sought of them. It is certainly wonderful that the princes especially and the cities have allowed this error to be agitated in their dominions, which has been condemned so often before in the Church, since eleven hundred years ago St. Jerome vanquished in this area the heretic Vigilantius. Long after him arose the Albigenses, the Poor Men of Lyons, the Picards, the Cathari old and new: all of whom were condemned legitimately long ago. Wherefore this article of the Confession, so frequently condemned, must be utterly rejected and in harmony with the entire universal Church be condemned; for in favor of the invocation of saints we have not only the authority of the Church universal but also the agreement of the holy fathers, Augustine, Bernard, Jerome, Cyprian, Chrysostom, Basil, and this class of other Church teachers. *[Reformers say that no human "works" can have an impact in the heavenly realm, but the* Confutatio *here reinforces the ties between heaven and earth, insisting that prayers offered through saints are efficacious.]*

Neither is the authority of Holy Scripture absent from this Catholic assertion, for Christ taught that the saints should be honored: "If any man serve me, him will my Father honor," John 12:26. If, therefore, God honors saints, why do not we, insignificant men, honor them? Besides, the Lord was turned to repentance by Job when he prayed for his friends, Job 42:8. Why, therefore, would not God, the most pious, who gave assent to Job, do the same to the Blessed Virgin when she intercedes? We read also in Baruch 3:4: "O Lord Almighty, thou God of Israel, hear now the prayers of the dead Israelites." Therefore the dead also pray for us. Thus did Onias and Jeremiah in the **Old Testament**. For Onias the high priest was seen by Judas Maccabaeus holding up his hands and praying for the whole body of the Jews. Afterwards another man appeared, remarkable both for his age and majesty, and of great beauty about him, concerning whom Onias replied: "This is a love of the brethren and of the people Israel, who prayeth much for the people and for the Holy city—to wit, Jeremiah the prophet." 2 Macc*[abees]* 15:12–14. Besides, we know from the Holy Scriptures that the angels pray for us. Why, then, would we deny this of the saints? "O Lord of hosts," said the angels, "how long wilt thou not have mercy on Jerusalem and on the cities of Judah, against which thou hast had indignation? And the Lord answered the angel that talked with me comfortable words." Zech. 1:12, 13.

Christ is our chief Advocate, and indeed the greatest; but since the saints are members of Christ, 1 Cor. 12:27 and Eph. 5:30, and conform their will to that of Christ, and see that their Head, Christ, prays for us, who can doubt that the saints do the very same thing which they see Christ doing? With all these things carefully considered, we must ask the princes and the cities adhering to them that they reject this part of the Confession and agree with the holy universal and orthodox Church and believe and confess, concerning the worship and intercession of saints, what the entire Christian world believes and confesses, and was observed in all the churches in the time of Augustine. "A Christian people," he says, "celebrates the memories of martyrs with religious observance, that it share in their merits and be aided by their prayers."

Defense to Article XXII [Of Lay Communion under One Form]

As in the Confessions of the princes and cities they enumerate among the abuses that laymen commune only under one form, and as, therefore, in their dominions both forms are administered to laymen, we must reply, according to the custom of the Holy Church, that this is incorrectly enumerated among the abuses, but that, according to the sanctions and statutes of the same Church, it is rather an abuse and disobedience to administer to laymen both forms. *[There are two "forms" of communion in the Lord's Supper: the bread and the wine. Reformers want ordinary people to partake of both, but the* Confutatio *explains here that the bread alone is sufficient for the laity.]*

For under the one form of bread the saints communed in the primitive Church, of whom Luke says: "They continued steadfastly in the apostles' doctrine and fellowship, and in breaking of bread." Acts 2:42. Here Luke mentions bread alone. Likewise Acts 20:7 says: "Upon the first day of the week, when the disciples came together to break bread." Yea, Christ, the institutor of this most holy sacrament, rising again from the dead, administered the Eucharist only under one form to the disciples going to Emmaus, where he took bread and blessed it, and brake and gave to them, and they recognized him in the breaking of bread. Luke 24:30, 31: where indeed Augustine, Chrysostome, Theophylact and Bede, some of whom many ages ago and not long after the times of the apostles, affirm that it was the Eucharist. Christ also (John 6) very frequently mentions bread alone. St. Ignatius, a disciple of St. John the Evangelist, in his Epistle to the Ephesians mentions the bread alone in the communion of the Eucharist. Ambrose does likewise in his books concerning the sacraments, speaking of the communion of Laymen. In the Council of Rheims, laymen were forbidden from bearing the sacrament of the Body to the sick, and no mention is there made of the form of wine. Hence it is understood that the viaticum was given the sick under only one form. The ancient penitential canons approve of this. For the Council of Agde put a guilty priest into a monastery and granted him only lay communion. In the Council of Sardica, Hosius prohibits certain indiscreet persons from receiving even lay communion, unless they finally repent.

There has always been a distinction in the Church between lay communion under one form and priestly communion under both forms. This was beautifully predicted in the Old Testament concerning the descendants of Eli: "It shall come to pass," says God, 1 Kings 2; 1 Sam. 2:36, "that everyone that is left in thine house shall come and crouch to him for a piece of silver and a morsel of bread, and shall say, 'Put me, I pray thee, into one of the priests' office.'" (Vulgate reads: *Ad unam partem sacerdotalem*— "that I may eat a piece of bread.") Here Holy Scripture clearly shows that the posterity of Eli, when removed from the office of the priesthood, will seek to be admitted to one sacerdotal part, to a piece of bread. So our laymen also ought, therefore, to be content with one sacerdotal part, the one form. For both the Roman pontiffs and cardinals and all bishops and priests, save in the mass and in the extreme hour of life for a viaticum, as it is called in the Council of Nice, are content with taking one form, which they would not do if they thought that both forms would be necessary for salvation. Although, however, both forms were of old administered in many churches to laymen (for then it was free to commune under one or under both forms), yet on account of many dangers the custom of administering both forms has ceased. For when the multitude of the people is considered where there are old and young, tremulous and weak and inept, if great care be not employed and injury is done the Sacrament by the spilling of the liquid. Because of the great multitude there would be difficulty also in giving the chalice cautiously for the form of wine, which also when kept for a long time would sour and cause nausea or vomition to those who would receive it; neither could it be readily taken to the sick without danger of spilling.

For these reasons and others the churches in which the custom had been to give both forms to laymen were induced, undoubtedly by impulse of the Holy Ghost, to give thereafter but one form, from the consideration chiefly that the entire Christ is under each form, and is received no less under one form than under two.

Therefore the princes and cities should be admonished to pay customary reverence and due honor to Christ the Son of the living God, our Savior and Glorifier, the Lord of heaven and earth, since they believe and acknowledge that he is truly present—a matter which they know has been most religiously observed by their ancestors, most Christian princes.

Defense to Article XXIII [Of the Marriage of Priests]

Their enumeration among abuses, in the second place, of the celibacy of the clergy, and the manner in which their priests marry and persuade others to marry, are verily matters worthy of astonishment, since they call sacerdotal celibacy an abuse, when that which is directly contrary, the violation of celibacy and the illicit transition to marriage, deserves to be called the worst abuse in priests. For that priests ought never to marry Aurelius testifies in the second Council of Carthage, where he says: "Because the apostles taught thus by example, and antiquity itself has preserved it, let us also maintain it." And a little before a canon to this effect is read: "Resolved, That the bishops, priests and deacons, or those who administer the sacraments, abstain, as guardians of chastity, from wives." From these words it is clear that this tradition has been received from the apostles, and not recently devised by the Church. Augustine, following Aurelius in the last question concerning the Old and New Testaments, writes upon these words, and asks: "If perhaps it be said, if it is lawful and good to marry, why are not priests permitted to have wives?" Pope Caliztus, a holy man and a martyr, decided thirteen hundred years ago that priests should not marry. The like is read also in the holy Councils of Caesarea, Neocaesarea, Africa, Agde, Gironne, Meaux, and Orleans. Thus the custom has been observed from the time of the Gospel and the apostles that one who has been put into the office of priests has never been permitted, according to law, to marry.

It is indeed true that on account of lack of ministers of God in the primitive Church married men were admitted to the priesthood, as is clear from the Apostolic Canons and the reply of Paphnutius in the Council of Nice; nevertheless, those who wished to contract marriage were compelled to do so before receiving the subdiaconate. This custom of the primitive Church the Greek Church has preserved and retained to this day. But when, by the grace of God, the Church has increased so that there was no lack of ministers in the Church, Pope Siricius, eleven hundred and forty years ago, undoubtedly not without the Holy Ghost, enjoined absolute continence upon the priests, Canon Plurimus, Dist. 82—an injunction which Popes Innocent I., Leo the Great and Gregory the Great approved and ratified, and which the Latin Church has everywhere observed to this day. From these facts it is regarded sufficiently clear that the celibacy of the clergy is not an abuse, and that it was approved by fathers so holy at such a remote time, and was received by the entire Latin Church. Besides, the priests of the old law, as in the case of Zacharias, were separated from their wives at times when they discharged their office and ministered in the temple. But since the priest of the new law ought always to be engaged in the ministry, it follows that he ought always to be continent. Furthermore, married persons should not defraud one the other of conjugal duties except for a time that they may give themselves to prayer. 1 Cor. 7:5. But since a priest ought always to pray, he ought always to be continent. Besides, St. Paul says: "But I would have you without carefulness. He that is unmarried careth for the things that belong to the Lord, that he may please the Lord. But he that is married careth for the things that are of the world, how he may please his wife," 1 Cor. 7:32–33.

For as to what Paul says, 1 Cor. 7:2: "To avoid fornication, let every man have his own wife," Jerome replies that St. Paul is speaking of one who has not made a vow, as Athanasius and Vulgarius understand the declaration of St. Paul: "If a virgin marry, she hath not sinned." (1 Cor. 7:28), that here a virgin is meant who has not been consecrated to God. So in reference to: "It is better to marry than to burn" (1 Cor. 7:9), the pointed reply of Jerome against Jovinian is extant. For the same St. Paul says (1 Cor. 7:1): "It is good for a man not to touch a woman." For a priest has the intermediate position of neither marrying nor burning, but of restraining himself by the grace of God, which he obtains of God by devout prayer and chastising of the flesh, by fasting and vigils.

Furthermore, when they say that Christ taught that all men are not fit for celibacy, it is indeed true, and on this account not all are fit for the priesthood; but let the priest pray, and he will be able to receive Christ's word concerning continence, as St. Paul says: "I can do all things through Christ which strengtheneth me," Phil. 4:13. Besides, when they allege that this is God's ordinance and command, Gen. 1:28, Jerome replied concerning these words a thousand years ago: "It was necessary first to plant the forest, and that it grow, in order that that might be which could afterwards be cut down." Then the command was given concerning the procreation of offspring, that the earth should be replenished, but since it has been replenished so that there is a pressure of nations, the commandment does not pertain in like manner upon those able to be continent.

In vain, too, do they boast of God's express order. Let them show, if they can, where God has enjoined priests to marry. Besides, we find in the divine law that vows once offered should be paid, Psalm. 49 and 75; Eccles. 5, Psalm. 50:14, 76:11; Eccles. 5:4. Why, therefore, do they not observe this express divine law? They also pervert St. Paul, as though he teaches that one who is to be chosen bishop should be married when he says: "Let a bishop be the husband of one wife"; which is not to be understood as though he ought to be married, for then Martin, Nicolaus, Titus, John the Evangelist, yea Christ, would not have been bishops. Hence Jerome explains the words of St. Paul, "that a bishop be the husband of one wife," as meaning that he be not a bigamist.

St. Paul said aright that the doctrine of those who forbid marriage is a doctrine of demons. Such was the doctrine of Tatian and Marcoin, whom Augustine and Jerome have mentioned. But the Church does not thus forbid marriage, as she even enumerates marriage among the seven sacraments; with which, however, it is consistent that on account of their superior ministry she should enjoin upon ecclesiastics superior purity. For it is false that there is an express charge concerning contracting marriage, for then John the Evangelist, St. James, Laurentius, Titus, Martin, Catharine, Barbara, etc., would have sinned. Nor is Cyprian influenced by these considerations to speak of a virgin who had made a solemn vow, but of one who had determined to live continently, as the beginning of Letter XI, Book I, sufficiently shows. For the judgement of St. Augustine is very explicit: "It is damnable for virgins who make a vow not only to marry, but even to wish to marry." Hence the abuse of marriage and the breaking of vows in the clergy are not to be tolerated.

Defense to Article XXVI [Of the Distinction of Meats]

What they afterwards assert concerning the distinction of meats and like traditions, of which they seem to make no account, must be rejected. For we know from the apostle that all power is of God, and especially that ecclesiastical power has been given by God for edification: for this reason, from the Christian and devout heart of the holy Church the constitutions of the same holy, catholic and apostolic Church should be received as are useful to the Church, as well for promoting divine worship as for restraining the lust of the flesh, while they enable us the more readily to keep the divine commands. . . . He says to the Corinthians very clearly: "But to the rest speak I, not the Lord." 1 Cor. 7.12, and again he says elsewhere: "Stand fast and hold the traditions which ye have been taught, whether by word or our epistle." 2 Thess. 2:15.

Wherefore, the princes and cities must be admonished to render obedience to ecclesiastical statutes and constitutions, lest when they withdraw obedience that is due God, obedience may be withdrawn also from them by their subjects, as their subjects attempted in the recent civil insurrection, not to allow themselves to be seduced by false doctrines. Most false also is their declaration that the righteousness of faith is obscured by such ordinances; nay, he is rather mad and insane who would observe them without faith. For they are given to believers, and not to Turks or Ishmaelites. "For what have I to do to judge them that are without?" 1 Cor. 5:12. Moreover, in extolling here faith above all things they antagonize St. Paul, as we have said above, and do violence to St. Paul, whom they pervert to evangelical works when he speaks of legal works, as all these errors have been above refuted. False also is it that ecclesiastical ordinances obscure God's commands, since they prepare man for these, as fasts suppress the lust of the flesh and help him from falling into luxury. False also is it that it is impossible to observe ordinances, for the Church is not a cruel mother who makes no exceptions in the celebration of festivals and in fasting and the like.

Paul (Col. 2) forbids that any one be judged in meat or in drink, or in respect to the Sabbath, after the Jewish manner; for when the Church forbids meats it does not judge them to be unclean, as the Jews in the Synagogue thought. So the declaration of Christ concerning that which goeth into the mouth (Matt. 15:11) is cited here without a sure and true understanding of it, since its intention was to remove the error of the Jews, who thought that food touched by unwashen hands becomes unclean, and rendered one eating it unclean, as is manifest from the context. Nor does the Church bring back to these observances Moses with his heavy hands.

Conclusion

From the foregoing—viz. the Confession and its Reply—since His Imperial Majesty perceives that the Elector, the princes and the cities agree on many points with the Catholic and Roman Church, and dissent from the godless dogmas that are disseminated all over Germany, and the pamphlets circulated everywhere, and that they disapprove of and condemn them,—His Holy Imperial Majesty is fully convinced, and hopes that the result will be, that when the Elector, princes and cities have heard and understood this Reply they will agree with united minds in regard to those matters also in which they perhaps have not agreed hitherto with the Roman Catholic Church, and that in all other things above mentioned they will obediently conform to the Catholic and Roman Church and the Christian faith and religion. For such conduct on their part His Imperial Majesty will be peculiarly grateful and will bestow his special favor upon them all in common, and also, as opportunity offers, upon them individually. For (which may God forbid) if this admonition, so Christian and indulgent, be unheeded, the Elector, princes and cities can judge that a necessary cause is afforded His Imperial Majesty that, as becometh a Roman Emperor and Christian Caesar and a defender and advocate of the Catholic and Christian Church, he must care for such matters as the nature of the charge committed to him and his integrity of conscience require.

SUPPLEMENTARY TEXTS

Ulrich Zwingli, *Of the Clarity and Certainty of the Word of God* (1522)

Like Luther, Zwingli appeals to scripture as the ultimate authority. But Zwingli recognizes that scripture alone is not enough. Passages from the Bible need to be understood in context and carefully analyzed with the help of the Holy Ghost. In this treatise, Zwingli explains the process by which one may come to properly understand scripture.

Source: S. M. Jackson, *Huldreich Zwingli: The Reformer of German Switzerland (1484–1531)* (Philadelphia: University of Pennsylvania Press, 1901).

By the Gospel we do not mean only the writings of Matthew, Mark, Luke and John, but, as we have said, all that God has revealed to man in order that he may instruct him and give him a sure knowledge of his will. But God is one, and he is a Spirit of unity, not of discord. Hence we may see that his words have always a true and natural sense; may God grant it, no matter how we may wrest them this way or that. And here I beg you in the name of God not to take it amiss if I draw your attention to a common error. It is that of the majority of those who in these days oppose the Gospel—for although they dare not admit to doing this in public, in secret they do everything within their power to that end. Listen to what they say. Not everything, they say, is told us in the Gospels. There are many good things which are never even thought of in the Gospel.

Oh you rascals—you are not instructed or versed in the Gospel, and you pick out verses from it without regard to their context, and wrest them according to your own desire. It is like breaking off a flower from its roots and trying to plant it in a garden. But that is not the way: you must plant it with the roots and the soil in which it is embedded. And similarly we must leave the Word of God its own proper nature if its sense is to be the same to all of us. And those who err in this way we can easily vanquish by leading them back to the source, though they never come willingly. But some of them are such confirmed dunces that even when the natural case is expounded in such a way that they cannot deny it, they still allege that they cannot presume to understand it thus unless the Fathers allow that it may so be understood.

The doctrine of God can never be learned with greater certainty than when it is taught by God himself, for it comes from God, and he alone is truthful, indeed, he is the truth itself. . . . Put away that view of your own which you want to read into Scripture, for it is quite valueless, as I shall clearly show. I know that you will reply that you have worked through the Scriptures and discovered texts which support your opinion. Alas! here we come upon the canker at the heart of all human systems. And it is this: we want to find support in Scripture for our own view, and so we take that view to Scripture, and if we find a text which, however artificially, we can relate to it, we do so, and in that way we wrest Scripture in order to make it say what we want it to say. . . .

If you want to speak on any matter, or to learn of it, you must first think like this: Before I say anything or listen to the teaching of man, I will first consult the mind of the Spirit of God (Psalm 84: "I will hear what God the Lord will speak.") Then you should reverently ask God for his grace, that he may give you his mind and Spirit, so that you will not lay hold of your own opinion but of his. And have a firm trust that he will teach you a right understanding, for all wisdom is of God the Lord. And then go to the written word of the Gospel. . . . You must be *theodidacti*, that is, taught of God, not of men: that is what the Truth itself said (John 6), and it cannot lie. If you do not believe, and believe firmly, leaving the wisdom of men and resting only in the divine instruction, you have no true faith. Thus the whole philosophical system called *theologica scholastica* falls to the ground, for it is merely a system evolved by man; and if it occupies the mind of a man, he thinks that the divine teaching is to be judged and perverted in accordance with the infallible teaching received of men. *[For Zwingli, scripture itself is not sufficient.*

To interpret it correctly requires grace or the Spirit of God.]

Today worldly or human wisdom is confounded and overthrown by those who have attained to the divine doctrine by inward longing and faith. We see, then, that the simplicity of the disciples was instructed only by God, which is an example to us, that we might seek the form of divine doctrine from God alone. The doctrine of God is never formed more clearly than when it is done by God himself and in the words of God. Indeed, I make bold to say that those who make themselves, that is men, the arbiters of Scripture, make a mockery of trust in the Spirit of God by their design and pretension, seeking to wrest and force the Scriptures according to their own folly. . . .

When I was younger, I gave myself overmuch to human teaching, like others of my day, and when about seven or eight years ago I undertook to devote myself entirely to the Scriptures I was always prevented by philosophy and theology. But eventually I came to the point where led by the Word and Spirit of God I saw the need to set aside all these things and to learn the doctrine of God direct from his own Word. Then I began to ask God for light and the Scriptures became far clearer to me—even though I read nothing else—than if I had studied many commentators and expositors. Note that that is always a sure sign of God's leading, for I could never have reached that point by my own feeble understanding. . . . And I am certain that that is the teaching of God, and you will not change my view even if you bring against me all the lies and inventions of the canonists or the hypocrisy of the monks or the wrath of the bloated prelates or the poison of Rome or the fire of Etna or indeed of hell itself. . . .

Amen.

Johann Maier von Eck, *Enchiridion of Commonplaces and Articles on the New Teachings* (1525), Selections

Johann Maier von Eck was one of Luther's first and most stalwart opponents, a brilliant theologian who defended the church and the pope against all the challenges of the reformers. Eck published an attack on Luther's 95 Theses *very soon after it appeared, then continued to engage Luther and other Wittenberg and Swiss reformers through printed pamphlets and fiery public disputations. Eck's* Enchiridion of Commonplaces *formulated a comprehensive defense of the Roman church; it went through forty-six editions between 1525 and 1576. In the* Enchiridion, *Eck refers to Old and New Testament scripture as well as the writings of important early church leaders such as Origen, Ambrose, Ignatius, and Chrysostom. The "heretics" and "new Christians" whom Eck argues against are the reformers: Swiss, Wittenberg, and Anabaptist.*

Source: Johann Maier von Eck, *Enchiridion: Handbüchlein gemainer stell unnd Articket der jetzt schwebenden Neuwen leeren* (Augsburg, 1533). Translation by Emily Fisher Gray.

Chapter 10. On the Eucharist in Both Forms

It is sufficient for the laity to receive the sacrament in one form. "The true bread . . . is that which comes down from heaven and gives life to the world" (John 6:33). "I am the living bread which came down from heaven" (John 6:41, 51). "And the bread that I will give is my flesh, for the life of the world" (John 6:52). In these cases, the Lord was only thinking about bread. When the two disciples were going to Emmaus (Luke 24:30), the Lord gave them the sacrament only in the form of bread, as Augustine and Chrysostom testified. Daily we pray, "Give us this day our daily bread" (Matt. 6:11). *["Both forms" refers to both the bread and the wine shared at the Last Supper. Traditionally, only priests consume the blessed wine.]*

OBJECTIONS OF THE NEW CHRISTIANS
- Christ established this sacrament under two forms and gave both to His apostles, commanding everyone, "All of you, drink of this" (Matt. 26:27).
- In the earliest churches the laity received both forms.
- It is commanded that one must eat the flesh of the Son of Man and drink his blood to be able to have life in Him.

RESPONSE OF THE CHRISTIANS
- We agree that Christ established the sacrament in two forms, and in our day consecrated priests should partake of both forms when they celebrate the Eucharist. This is how the apostles took the sacrament; they were priests, too. When Christ told his apostles to drink in remembrance of Him, there were no laypeople present.
- We admit that in the beginning of the church the laity received the sacrament in both forms, but since then much has changed.
  — Considering the many kinds of people present—very old, very young, clumsy—if any of them did not take great care, it is possible that the sacrament could be desecrated through the spilling of the liquid.
  — There would have to be a very large quantity of wine available.
  — It is possible that the wine could make people sick if it turns to vinegar or goes bad and loses its taste, and people could become nauseated.
- Sacramental eating is spiritual eating. "The words that I have spoken are spirit and life" (John 6:64). The whole of Christ exists in each form, so the laity partakes in both the flesh and blood of Christ under the form of the bread.... The priest partakes of both the bread and wine on behalf of the whole church and all of the people. Thus all of the people, in a spiritual sense, with joyful faith, drink the blood of Christ.

Chapter 11: On the Sacrament of Marriage

We will prove that the law of the Gospel establishes marriage as a sacrament. "Women are to be subject to their husbands, as to the Lord, because the husband is the head of the wife, just as Christ is the head of the church" (Eph. 5:22). Later, "On this account a man will leave his father and mother, and cleave unto his wife, and the two will be one flesh: this is a great sacrament, that I speak in Christ and the church" (Eph. 5:31–32). Thus Paul openly announced that marriage was a sacrament, because the joining of man and wife also represents the relationship between Christ and the church.

OBJECTIONS OF THE NEW CHRISTIANS
- St. Paul says that marriage is a sacrament, but in Greek this is translated as "mystery."
- He says that it is a great sacrament only with respect to the relationship between Christ and the church.

RESPONSE OF THE CHRISTIANS
- It is true that marriage is a mystery, but only a heretic would say that it should not therefore be a sacrament. All sacraments are mysteries, which is why the Greeks named the sacraments *mysteria*.
- It is true that marriage is a symbol Christ and the church, but it is nonetheless a sacrament in and of itself—for a sacrament is a sign of holy things. Paul explains that marriage is a sign of the union of Christ and the church, and also of grace.

Chapter 14: On Feasts and Fast Days

The church has established that certain foods can be prohibited. "You are to abstain from things sacrificed to idols and from blood and things strangled" (Acts 15:29). "All things indeed are clean, but it is evil for that man who eats with offence. It is good not to eat flesh and not to drink wine, nor anything by which your brother is made weak or scandalized" (Rom. 14:19–21). "Flesh and wine have not entered into my mouth" (Dan. 10:3). "But you, when you fast, anoint your head and wash your face in order that you may not seem to men to be fasting but to your Father who is in secret, and your Father who sees in secret will repay you" (Matt. 6:17). Pope Leo IV said it is an ancient custom not to eat meat on Wednesdays and Fridays.

Jesus fasted forty days and forty nights, and afterward he was hungry (Matt. 4:2). Moses likewise fasted forty days (Deut. 9:9). Fasting makes one holy; the soul is humbled in fasting. St. Jerome said, "Do not hold the forty days fast *[of Lent]* for nothing, for it contains an imitation of the journey of God." Pope Telesphorus, who lived near to the apostles' time, confirmed this, as did Ambrose in many sermons and the Councils of Agathen and Aurelianen. Origen, in his tenth homily on Leviticus, said that we have sanctified the forty days *[of Lent]* with fasting. Jerome said that we fast forty days in the year according to the tradition of the apostles.

OBJECTIONS OF THE HERETICS
- "It is not what enters the mouth that defiles a man" (Matt. 15:11).
- "Let no man therefore judge you in food, or in drink, or in respect of a festival day, or of the new moon, or of the sabbaths, which are a shadow of things to come" (Col. 2:16).
- Christ in the Gospels never issued commandments about the choice of foods; why lay this burden upon Christians?
- Christian freedom does not allow these burdens of servitude (Acts 15:28).

ANSWERS OF THE FAITHFUL
- Christ says nothing about fasting here *[in Matt. 15:11]*, but is correcting an error of the Jews, who thought that foods touched with unwashed hands were made unclean and those who ate became unclean also.
- The apostle did not want us to follow the Jewish traditions that certain foods were always forbidden such as pork. . . . The church believes that all meats are good at the right times.
- Christ may not have taught that man should sometimes abstain from meats; he taught more essential things. But many things conducive to salvation he leaves to the church and the **Holy Spirit** to teach. As he said, "I have many things to say to you, but you cannot bear them now" (John 16:12). He also did not forbid circumcision, but we do not see a lot of New Christians practicing that.

Chapter 16: Concerning the Images of Christ and of the Saints

Although the Jewish people were inclined toward **idolatry**, still God commanded them to create some images. "You shall make also two cherubim of beaten gold on the two sides of the oracle. Let one cherub be on the one side and the other on the other" (Exod. 25:18). "The Lord said to Moses: make a brazen serpent and set it up for a sign" (Num. 21:8).

John of Damascus testifies that Christians are able to use images because this custom was instituted by the apostles. Eusebius and John of Damascus both write that Christ sent an image of Himself to Abgar, the king of Edessa, which is preserved in St. Bartholomew's church in Genoa. The Lord also gave a handkerchief to St. Veronica imprinted with a likeness of his face, and this object healed King Tiberius.

Bede says there is no scripture that forbids the use of images in the church. Athanasius writes of a miracle that happened in Beirut with the Cross of Nicodemus, an image of the crucified. It follows therefore that images were used during the time of the apostles. Eusebius writes about images of Peter and Paul as well as images of Christ performing miracles. Charlemagne wrote four books against those who wished to destroy images; the people of Zurich should follow the example of this great ruler instead of the image-breaker Zwingli.

Images are useful. They instruct the simple, admonish the wise, wake up the lazy, and benefit everyone. It pleases God that to make Himself visible to us in human form, just as we are all visible to Him. Even Luther was wise in this respect when he saw Karlstadt destroying images and banned him from Saxony. Luther says that contemplative or testimonial images of Christ and the saints should be tolerated, and not only tolerated, but praised and honored when they promote remembrance and faith.

OBJECTIONS OF THE NEW CHRISTIANS
- "You shall not make a graven image or a likeness of anything which is in heaven above, on earth below, or of those things which are in waters under the earth" (Exod. 20:4).
- King Hezekiah destroyed the brazen serpent of Moses (2 Kings 18:4).
- Christ promised that the time will come—and the time is now—that supplicants will approach God in spirit and truth, but the Holy Spirit does not come through images.
- Images present a danger of idolatry and unclean thoughts.

REPLY OF THE CHRISTIANS
- God forbade the worship of foreign gods and also images of them. But the saints are not gods; therefore, images of them are not forbidden.
- Hezekiah had the brazen serpent destroyed because of its misuse by the people, who made it into an idol. Until that time the children of Israel had worshipped correctly. Therefore, if an image is misused, it should be done away with, but the problem is the idolatry—not the image itself.
- God must be worshipped in spirit and truth, and images can admonish and remind us to do this. The spirit does not reject physical signs; the sacraments are also physical and visible symbols.
- There is no danger of idolatry, because the common man can be taught so that he has a good understanding and should not honor the image itself, which is made of wood or stone, but rather what the image represents. Images of lascivious subjects should not be brought into the church.

Chapter 19: Concerning the Marriage of Priests
God has commanded priests that they should be holy so they can participate in the sacrifice of the Mass. How can Luther allow his priests to consort with women and whores and then consecrate the Living Bread that comes down from heaven in true form of the body of Christ?

He that is without a wife is solicitous for the things that belong to the Lord and concerned about how he may please God. But he that is with a wife is solicitous for the things of the world, thinking about how he may please his wife, and his heart is divided (1 Cor. 7:32–34). Paul warns the married that for a time they abstain from the marriage bed that they may be more open to prayer (1 Cor. 7:5). Priests should always stand by their altars and therefore must remain unmarried. More than 1,300 years ago Pope Calixtus forbade priests, deacons, presbyters, and monks to have wives. Augustine said that it is good for a man to marry, but not for a priest.

OBJECTIONS OF THE NEW CHRISTIANS
- The priests in the Old Testament had wives.
- God has commanded man to increase and multiply (Gen. 1:22).
- St. Paul says it is better to marry than to burn (1 Cor. 7:9).

REPLY OF THE CHRISTIANS
- Ambrose answers that the priests and Levites of the Old Testament had wives because they had plenty of time free from their priestly duties. There were many priests, and they did not all serve at the same time, according to practices established by King David. But all priests had to abstain from relations with women while they were in the service of God. Also, only Levites could serve as priests, so they had wives to perpetuate the lineage of Levi, otherwise they would become extinct.
- God commanded men to fill the earth, but now men should concentrate on filling the heavens, because there are plenty of children on earth. This commandment was not meant to be permanent, otherwise John the Baptist would be a sinner for remaining a virgin, and also Mary, and St. Paul would be in error for counseling virginity, and Christ would not have praised eunuchs (Matt. 19:12).

Chapter 37: That Masses Are to Be Said in Latin, Not in German

The reasonable custom of the church is to use Latin Mass in the Latin church. It would create great confusion, that when Italians, Spaniards, French, English, Hungarians, Bohemians, etc. come to us, they would not understand the action of the Mass, and all would seem to be barbarians to one another. The Mass would be held in contempt. And not only would confusion occur between diverse nations, but also scandal would be caused in the same nation. For in Germany itself, some use one word, others another, and what in one district means something honorable, in another it means something filthy. And diversity of pronunciation in Germany would lead to such great dissonance that it would be more confused than in Babylon.

A greater irreverence would be done to the mystery if it were carried out in the common speech, such that it would be made fun of at the crossroads and in the barbershops and at banquets, as now happens in Lutheran places.

Therefore, it is quite enough in the Catholic Church for the Mass to be read in Latin and Greek languages, for the generality of peoples who have entered the church in these two languages have distinguished themselves in wisdom and power.

OBJECTIONS OF THE HERETICS

- Paul forbids the Corinthians to speak in church in a language that is not understood, for he says, "How shall he say amen to your blessing, because he does not know what you are saying?" (1 Cor. 14:16). Now if the Mass is read in Latin, the laymen do not understand it. And thus the hearing of it bears no fruit, as if the sermon were delivered to a wall.

RESPONSE OF THE CHRISTIANS

- Anyone would in vain preach to Germans in an unknown language, but of the Mass Paul makes no mention. This is clear form Paul's words: "But in the church I had rather speak five words with my understanding, that I may instruct others also" (1 Cor. 14:19). Ponder "I may instruct," which is done by preaching, not be celebration of the Mass.
- And if the laity do not understand the words, they at least understand all mysteries, which they imbibed from their childhood or the teaching of their parents. Therefore, now with kneeling, now with rising, now with making the sign of the cross, they accommodate themselves to the celebration of the Mass. Hence this outward action shows they understand more of the mystery of the Mass than if Cicero, Livy, and Varro—most learned in the Latin language, but not instructed concerning the mystery—heard the words.

Let us therefore conclude: the Latin Mass is enough for Germans, since they are the Latin church, and we ought to reverently recognize the mysteries of the Savior under this practice and the greatness of the mystery as Augustine, Alcuin, Isidore, Bede, and others attest.

Martin Luther, *Against the Heavenly Prophets in the Matter of Images and Sacraments* (1525)

Martin Luther wrote a treatise in response to Andreas Karlstadt von Bodenstein, who advocated the immediate and thorough removal of all images from the churches in Wittenberg. Luther worried about the potential violence and disorder if the removal of images turned into rampant iconoclasm—just as Luther worried about Karlstadt's implicit challenge to his authority as the leader of the Wittenberg reformers.

Source: Conrad Bergendorff, ed., *Luther's Works*, vol. 40, trans. Bernhard Erling (Minneapolis: Augsburg Fortress, 1958).

I approached the task of destroying images by first tearing them out of the heart through God's Word and making them worthless and despised! For when they are no longer in the heart, they can do no harm when seen with the eyes. But Dr. Karlstadt, who pays no attention to matters of the heart, has reversed the order by removing them from sight and leaving them in the heart!

I have allowed and not forbidden the outward removal of images, so long as this takes place without rioting and uproar and is done by the proper authorities! And I say at the outset that according to the law of Moses no other images are forbidden than an image of God which one worships. A crucifix, on the other hand, or any other holy image is not forbidden. Heigh now! You breakers of images, I defy you to prove the opposite! Thus we read that Moses's Brazen Serpent remained (Num. 21:8) until Hezekiah destroyed it solely because it had been worshiped (II Kings 18:4)

However, to speak evangelically of images, I say and declare that no one is obligated to break violently images even of God, but everything is free, and one does not sin if he does not break them with violence!

Nor would I condemn those who have destroyed them, especially those who destroy divine and idolatrous images. But images for memorial and witness, such as crucifixes and images of saints, are to be tolerated. This is shown above to be the case even in the Mosaic law. And they are not only to be tolerated, but for the sake of the memorial and the witness they are praiseworthy and honorable, as the witness stones of Joshua (Josh. 24:26) and of Samuel (I Sam. 7:12).

The Schleitheim Confession of Faith (1527)

Leaders of several Anabaptist groups came together in the town of Schleitheim in February 1527 and reached consensus on several major issues, including the nature of baptism and the Lord's Supper. This "confession" or statement of belief outlines seven principles on which Anabaptists largely agree.

Source: John Howard Yoder, ed., *The Legacy of Michael Sattler* (Walden, NY: Plough Publishing House, 2019). Used with permission.

The Seven Articles

The articles we have dealt with, and in which we have been united, are these: baptism, ban, the breaking of bread, separation from abomination, shepherds in the congregation, the sword, the oath.

I. Notice concerning baptism. Baptism shall be given to all those who have been taught repentance and the amendment of life and *[who]* believe truly that their sins are taken away through Christ, and to all those who desire to walk in the resurrection of Jesus Christ and be buried with Him in death, so that they might rise with Him; to all those who with such an understanding themselves desire and request it from us; hereby is excluded all infant baptism, the greatest and first abomination of the pope. For this you have the reasons and the testimony of the writings and the practice of the apostles. We wish simply yet resolutely and with assurance to hold to the same.

II. We have been united as follows concerning the ban. The ban shall be employed with all those who have given themselves over to the Lord, to walk after *[Him]* in His commandments; those who have been baptized into the one body of Christ, and let themselves be called brothers or sisters, and still somehow slip and fall into error and sin, being inadvertently overtaken. The same *[shall]* be warned twice privately and the third time be publicly admonished before the entire congregation according to the command of Christ (Matthew 18). But this shall be done according to the ordering of the Spirit of God before the breaking of bread so that we may all in one spirit and in one love break and eat from one bread and drink from one cup. *[The "ban" is ostracism of a wayward Anabaptist from the spiritual community.]*

III. Concerning the breaking of bread, we have become one and agree thus: all those who desire to break the one bread in remembrance of the broken body of Christ and all those who wish to drink of one drink in remembrance of the shed blood of Christ, they must beforehand be united in the one body of Christ, that is the congregation of God, whose head is Christ, and that by baptism. For as Paul indicates, we cannot be partakers at the same time of the table of the Lord and the table of devils. Nor can we at the same time partake and drink of the cup of the Lord and the cup of devils. That is: all those who have fellowship with the dead works of darkness have no part in the light. Thus all those who follow the devil and the world, have no part with those who have been called out of the world unto God. All those who lie in evil have no part in the good. *["The breaking of bread" is the way Anabaptists describe the Lord's Supper.]*

So it shall and must be, that whoever does not share the calling of the one God to one faith, to one baptism, to one spirit, to one body together with all the children of God, may not be made one loaf together with them, as must be true if one wishes truly to break bread according to the command of Christ.

IV. We have been united concerning the separation that shall take place from the evil and the wickedness which the devil has planted in the world, simply in this; that we have no fellowship with them, and do not run with them in the confusion of their abominations. So it is; since all who have not entered into the obedience of faith and have not united themselves with God so that they will to do His will, are a great abomination before God, therefore nothing else can or really will grow or spring forth from them than abominable things. Now there is nothing else in the world and all creation than good or evil, believing and unbelieving, darkness and light, the world and those who are *[come]* out of the world, God's temple and idols. Christ and Belial, and none will have part with the other.

To us, then, the commandment of the Lord is also obvious, whereby He orders us to be and to become separated from the evil one, and thus He will be our God and we shall be His sons and daughters. *[For Anabaptists, the separation from the "evil one" requires isolation from the broader Christian community.]*

Further, He admonishes us therefore to go out from Babylon and from the earthly Egypt, that we may not be partakers in their torment and suffering, which the Lord will bring upon them. From all this we should learn that everything which has not been united with our God in Christ is nothing but an abomination which we should shun. By this are meant all popish and re-popish works and idolatry, gatherings, church attendance, wine houses, guarantees and commitments of unbelief, and other things of the kind, which the world regards highly, and yet which are carnal or flatly counter to the command of God, after the pattern of all the iniquity which is in the world. From all this we shall be separated and have no part with such, for they are nothing but abominations, which cause us to be hated before our Christ Jesus, who has freed us from the servitude of the flesh and fitted us for the service of God and the Spirit whom He has given us.

Thereby shall also fall away from us the diabolical weapons of violence—such as sword, armor, and the like, and all of their use to protect friends or against enemies—by virtue of the word of Christ: "you shall not resist evil."

V. We have been united as follows concerning shepherds in the church of God. The shepherd in the church shall be a person according to the rule of Paul, fully and completely, who has a good report of those who are outside the faith. The office of such a person shall be to read and exhort and teach, warn, admonish, or ban in the congregation, and properly to preside among the sisters and brothers in prayer, and in the breaking of bread, and in all things to take care of the body of Christ, that it may be built up and developed, so that the name of God might be praised and honored through us, and the mouth of the mocker be stopped. *[The "shepherd" is an Anabaptist pastor or leader.]*

He shall be supported, wherein he has need, by the congregation which has chosen him, so that he who serves the gospel can also live therefrom, as the Lord has ordered. But should a shepherd do something worthy of reprimand, nothing shall be done with him without the voice of two or three witnesses.

If they sin they shall be publicly reprimanded, so that others might fear. But if the shepherd should be driven away or led to the Lord by the cross, at the same hour another shall be ordained to his place, so that the little folk and the little flock of God may not be destroyed, but be preserved by warning and be consoled.

VI. We have been united as follows concerning the sword. The sword is an ordering of God outside the perfection of Christ. It punishes and kills the wicked and guards and protects the good. In the law the sword is established over the wicked for punishment and for death, and the secular rulers are established to wield the same. *[Anabaptists were particularly noteworthy for their pacifism. Why would their refusal to use a weapon be a threat to the larger community?]*

But within the perfection of Christ only the ban is used for the admonition and exclusion of the one who has sinned, without the death of the flesh, simply the warning and the command to sin no more.

Now many, who do not understand Christ's will for us, will ask whether a Christian may or should use the sword against the wicked for the protection and defense of the good, or for the sake of love.

The answer is unanimously revealed: Christ teaches and commands us to learn from Him, for He is meek and lowly of heart and thus we shall find rest for our souls. Now Christ says to the woman who was taken in adultery, not that she should be stoned according to the law of His Father (and yet He says, "What the Father commanded me, that I do"), but with mercy and forgiveness and the warning to sin no more, says: "Go, sin no more." Exactly thus should we also proceed, according to the rule of the ban.

Second, is asked concerning the sword: whether a Christian shall pass sentence in disputes and strife about worldly matters, such as the unbelievers have with one another. The answer: Christ did not wish to decide or pass judgment between brother and brother concerning inheritance, but refused to do so. So should we also do.

Third, is asked concerning the sword: whether the Christian should be a magistrate if he is chosen thereto. This is answered thus: Christ was to be made king, but He fled and did not discern the ordinance of His Father. Thus we should also do as He did and follow after Him, and we shall not walk in darkness. For He Himself says: "Whoever would come after me, let him deny himself and take up his cross and follow me." He Himself further forbids the violence of the sword when He says: "The princes of this world lord it over them etc., but among you it shall not be so." Further Paul says, "Whom God has foreknown, the same he has also predestined to be conformed to the image of his Son," etc. Peter also says: "Christ has suffered (not ruled) and has left us an example, that you should follow after in his steps." Lastly, one can see in the following points that it does not befit a Christian to be a magistrate: the rule of the government is according to the flesh, that of the Christians according to the Spirit. Their houses and dwelling remain in this world, that of the Christians is in heaven. Their citizenship is in this world, that of the Christians is in heaven. The weapons of their battle and warfare are carnal and only against the flesh, but the weapons of Christians are spiritual, against the fortification of the devil. The worldly are armed with steel and iron, but Christians are armed with the armor of God, with truth, righteousness, peace, faith, salvation, and with the Word of God. In sum: as Christ our Head is minded, so also must be minded the members of the body of Christ through Him, so that there be no division in the body, through which it would be destroyed. Since then Christ is as is written of Him, so must His members also be the same, so that His body may remain whole and unified for its own advancement and upbuilding. For any kingdom which is divided within itself will be destroyed.

VII. We have been united as follows concerning the oath. The oath is a confirmation among those who are quarreling or making promises. In the law it is commanded that it should be done only in the name of God, truthfully and not falsely. Christ, who teaches the perfection of the law, forbids His *[followers]* all swearing, whether true or false; neither by heaven nor by earth, neither by Jerusalem nor by our head; and that for the reason which He goes on to give: "For you cannot make one hair white or black." You see, thereby all swearing is forbidden. We cannot perform what is promised in the swearing, for we are not able to change the smallest part of ourselves. . . . *[Anabaptists do not believe in swearing oaths (invoking God in making a promise to do something). Why might people think Anabaptists are untrustworthy?]*

Martin Luther, *The Small Catechism* (1529), Selections

Martin Luther found many people profoundly ignorant of what he considered the essentials of Christian faith, so he created a brief introduction to the most important doctrines of a reformed church. Pastors, parents, or teachers could use this text to instruct children in the Gospel. The sections on baptism and the Lord's Supper ("sacrament of the altar") are excerpted here.

Source: F. Bente, ed., *Triglot Concordia: The Symbolical Books of the Evangelical Lutheran Church: German-Latin-English* (St. Louis, MO: Concordia, 1921).

Baptism

THE NATURE OF BAPTISM

What is Baptism?

Baptism is not just water, but it is the water used according to God's command and connected with His Word.

What is that Word and command of God concerning Baptism?

Jesus says: "All authority has been given to Me in heaven and on earth. Go therefore and make disciples of all the nations, baptizing them in the name of the Father and of the Son and of the Holy Spirit, teaching them to observe all things whatever I have commanded you." Matthew 28:18–20.

THE BLESSINGS OF BAPTISM

What does Baptism give or profit?

Baptism effects forgiveness of sins, delivers from death and the devil, and gives eternal salvation to all who believe this, just as the words and promises of God declare.

Which are these words and promises of God?

Christ our Lord says, Mark 16:16: "He who believes and is baptized will be saved; but he who does not believe will be condemned."

THE POWER OF BAPTISM

How can water do such great things?

It is not the water that does these things, but the Word of God which is in and with the water, and faith which trusts this Word of God in the water. For without the Word of God the water is simply water, and no baptism; but with the Word of God it is a baptism, that is, a gracious water of life and washing of regeneration in the Holy Spirit, as St. Paul says, Titus 3:5–8: "According to His mercy He saved us, by the washing of regeneration and renewing of the Holy Spirit, whom He poured out on us abundantly through Jesus Christ our Savior; that having been justified by His grace, we should become heirs according to the hope of eternal life. This is a faithful saying."

THE MEANING OF BAPTISM

What does such baptizing with water mean?

Such baptizing with water means that the old Adam in us should, by daily contrition and repentance, be drowned and die with all sins and evil lusts; and that a new man daily come forth and arise, who shall live before God in righteousness and purity forever.

Where is this written?

St. Paul writes, Romans 6:4: "We are buried with Christ by baptism into death, that just as He was raised up from the dead by the glory of the Father, even so we also should walk in newness of life."

The Sacrament of the Altar

THE NATURE OF THE SACRAMENT OF THE ALTAR

What is the Sacrament of the Altar?

The Sacrament of the Altar is the true body and blood of our Lord Jesus Christ, under the bread and wine, instituted by Christ himself, for us Christians to eat and to drink.

Where is this written?

The holy evangelists Matthew, Mark, Luke, together with St. Paul, write thus: "Our Lord Jesus Christ, the same night in which He was betrayed, took bread; and when He had given thanks, He broke it and gave it to His disciples, saying, 'Take, eat; this is My body, which is given for you. Do this in remembrance of Me.' In the same way also He took the cup after supper, gave thanks and gave it to them, saying, 'Drink from it all of you; this cup is the New Testament in My blood, which is shed for you for the remission of sins. Do this, as often as you drink it, in remembrance of Me.'"

THE BENEFIT OF THE SACRAMENT OF THE ALTAR

What benefit do we receive from such eating and drinking?

The benefit which we receive from such eating and drinking is shown us by these words: "Given and shed for you for the remission of sins," namely, that in the Sacrament forgiveness of sins, life and salvation are given us through these words. For where there is forgiveness of sins, there is also life and salvation.

THE POWER OF THE SACRAMENT OF THE ALTAR

How can bodily eating and drinking do such great things?

It is not the eating and drinking that does this, but the words here written, "Given and shed for you for the remission of sins." These words, along with the eating and drinking, are the main thing in the Sacrament; and whoever believes these words has exactly what they say, namely, the forgiveness of sins.

THE PROPER RECEPTION OF THE SACRAMENT OF THE ALTAR

Who then receives this Sacrament worthily?

Fasting and bodily preparation are indeed a fine outward training; but he is truly worthy and well prepared who has faith in these words, "Given and shed for you for the remission of sins." But he who does not believe these words, or doubts them, is unworthy and unprepared; for the words "for you" require truly believing hearts.

Ulrich Zwingli, Letter to Vadian concerning the Marburg Colloquy (1529)

The Protestant-leaning Landgrave (Prince) Philip of Hesse invited Zwingli, Luther, Melanchthon, and Oecolampadius to Marburg to try to reach a unified Reformed agreement on major issues. The talks broke down almost immediately, with no one willing to make concessions. This letter gives Zwingli's account of the discussions over the meaning of the Eucharist.

Source: S. M. Jackson, *Huldreich Zwingli: The Reformer of German Switzerland (1484–1531)* (Philadelphia: University of Pennsylvania Press, 1901).

Grace and peace from the Lord.

I will now write briefly what you desire to know. After we had been brought under the safest conduct to Marburg, and Luther with his party had come, the Prince Landgrave determined that Oecolampadius and Luther, Melanchthon and Zwingli, should meet two by two in private to see whether they could not find some ground of agreement upon which they could found peace. Hereupon Luther received Oecolampadius in such a way that the latter came to me complaining secretly that he had met another Eck—but this is to be told to the trusty alone.

As for Melanchthon, he was so slippery and so transformed himself after the manner of Proteus that he compelled me to seize a pen, to arm my hand, and dry it as with salt and so hold him more firmly as he glided around in all sorts of escapes and subterfuges. . . . But I do not wish to give rise to a new quarrel. Philip and I were engaged in conversation for six hours, Luther and Oecolampadius for three. On the next day, in the presence of the Landgrave and twenty-four witnesses, Luther and Melanchthon and Oecolampadius and Zwingli went into the arena and fought there and in three other sessions. For there were four in all in which we contended successfully.

For we presented to Luther as needing explanation the fact that he had propounded those thrice foolish statements: that Christ suffered in His divine nature; that the Body of Christ is everywhere; and that the flesh could not profit of itself otherwise than as he now asserted. But the fine fellow made no reply, except that in the matter of the flesh not profiting he said: "You know, Zwingli, that as time progressed and their judgment grew, all the Fathers treated the passages of Scripture in ways different from the earlier expositions." Then he said: "The Body of Christ is eaten corporeally in our body, but in the meantime I will reserve this to myself whether the Body is eaten by the soul." And yet a little before he had said, "The Body of Christ is eaten with the mouth corporeally, the soul does not eat Him corporeally." He also said: "The Body of Christ is produced by these words, 'This is My Body,' no matter how wicked the man who pronounces these words." *[Zwingli pushes Luther on the issue of transubstantiation. The statement that the "flesh profits nothing" (John 6:63) means that human actions or "works" such as partaking of the Eucharist do not affect salvation.]*

He conceded that the Body of Christ is finite. He admitted that the Eucharist can be called the sign of the Body of Christ. These and other innumerable vacillating, absurd, and foolish utterances of his, which he babbled forth like pebbles on a beach, we so argued on that now the Prince himself is on our side, although for the sake of certain princes he pretended not to be. Almost all the Court of Hesse have deserted Luther. He himself grants that our books could be read without harm. Hereafter he will suffer the parties who agree with us to retain their positions. Prince John of Saxony was not present, but the Prince of Wittenberg was.

We parted with the understanding which you will see in print. Truth was so clearly superior that, if ever any one was overcome, Luther, the impudent and obstinate, was beaten, and before a wise and just judge, although meantime he was unconquered.

We have effected this good, that after we shall agree in the other dogmas of the Christian religion, the Pope's party cannot entertain the hope that Luther will be theirs. While I write this I am wearied with my journey; when you come to us you shall have a full report. For I think we have also gained something else; things that will prove a safeguard for religion and against the monarchy of Cæsar. These also shall be set forth to you when the time shall demand it. Meanwhile, farewell, and greet all friends.

Yours,
Huldreich Zwingli
Zurich, October 20, 1529.

Philip Melanchthon, *Apology of the Augsburg Confession* (1530), Selections

After presenting the Augsburg Confession *to the Diet of Augsburg, Philip Melanchthon began writing a more in-depth "apology" (explanation) of the major points of Wittenberg's approach to reformed doctrine. The presentation of the* Confutatio Pontificia *accelerated Melanchthon's work, and his* Apology of the Augsburg Confession *is in many ways a response to the* Confutatio, *which was a response to the original Augsburg Confession.*

Source: F. Bente, ed., *Triglot Concordia: The Symbolical Books of the Evangelical Lutheran Church: German-Latin-English* (St. Louis, MO: Concordia, 1921).

Article IX. Of Baptism

The Ninth Article has been approved, in which we confess that Baptism is necessary to salvation, and that children are to be baptized, and that the baptism of children is not in vain but is necessary and effectual to salvation. And since the Gospel is taught among us purely and diligently, by God's favor we receive also from it this fruit, that in our Churches no Anabaptists gained ground, because the people have been fortified by God's Word against the wicked and seditious faction of these robbers. [*This section provides a good explanation of why infants should be baptized—and hence why Anabaptists' insistence on adult baptism is dangerous and heretical.*]

And as we condemn quite a number of other errors of the Anabaptists, we condemn this also, that they dispute that the baptism of little children is profitable. For it is very certain that the promise of salvation pertains also to little children. It does not, however, pertain to those who are outside of Christ's Church, where there is neither Word nor Sacraments, because the kingdom of Christ exists only with the Word and Sacraments. Therefore it is necessary to baptize little children, that the promise of salvation may be applied to them, according to Christ's command, Matt. 28:19: Baptize all nations. Just as here salvation is offered to all, so Baptism is offered to all, to men, women, children, infants. It clearly follows, therefore, that infants are to be baptized, because with Baptism salvation (the universal grace and treasure of the Gospel) is offered.

Secondly, it is manifest that God approves of the baptism of little children. Therefore the Anabaptists, who condemn the baptism of little children, believe wickedly. That God, however, approves of the baptism of little children is shown by this, namely, that God gives the Holy Ghost to those thus baptized to many who have been baptized in childhood. For if this baptism would be in vain, the Holy Ghost would be given to none, none would be saved, and finally there would be no Church. For there have been many holy men in the Church who have not been baptized otherwise. This reason, even taken alone, can sufficiently establish good and godly minds against the godless and fanatical opinions of the Anabaptists.

Article X. Of the Lord's Supper

The Tenth Article has been approved, in which we confess that we believe, that in the Lord's Supper the body and blood of Christ are truly and substantially present, and are truly tendered, with those things which are seen, bread and wine, to those who receive the Sacrament. This belief we constantly defend, as the subject has been carefully examined and considered. For since Paul says, 1 Cor. 10:16, that the bread is the communion of the Lord's body, etc., it would follow, if the Lord's body were not truly present, that the bread is not a communion of the body, but only of the spirit of Christ. And we have ascertained that not only the Roman Church affirms the bodily presence of Christ, but the Greek Church also both now believes, and formerly believed, the same. For the canon of the Mass among them testifies to this, in which the priest clearly prays that the bread may be changed and become the very body of Christ.

And Vulgarius, who seems to us to be not a silly writer, says distinctly that bread is not a mere figure, but is truly changed into flesh. And there is a long exposition of Cyril on John 15, in which he teaches that Christ is corporeally offered us in the Supper. For he says thus: Nevertheless, we do not deny that we are joined spiritually to Christ by true faith and sincere love. But that we have no mode of connection with Him, according to the flesh, this indeed we entirely deny. And this, we say, is altogether foreign to the divine Scriptures. For who has doubted that Christ is in this manner a vine, and we the branches, deriving thence life for ourselves? Hear Paul saying 1 Cor. 10:17; Rom. 12:5; Gal. 3:28: We are all one body in Christ; although we are many, we are, nevertheless, one in Him; for we are, all partakers of that one bread. Does he perhaps think that the virtue of the mystical benediction is unknown to us? Since this is in us, does it not also, by the communication of Christ's flesh, cause Christ to dwell in us bodily? And a little after: Whence we must consider that Christ is in us not only according to the habit, which we call love, but also by natural participation, etc. *[Melanchthon clarifies here that whatever disagreements reformers have with the Roman church, they agree on the physical presence of God in the bread and wine of the Lord's Supper.]*

We have cited these testimonies, not to undertake a discussion here concerning this subject, for His Imperial Majesty does not disapprove of this article, but in order that all who may read them may the more clearly perceive that we defend the doctrine received in the entire Church, that in the Lord's Supper the body and blood of Christ are truly and substantially present, and are truly tendered with those things which are seen, bread and wine. And we speak of the presence of the living Christ; for we know that death hath no more dominion over Him, Rom. 6:9.

Article XV. Of Human Traditions in the Church

In the Fifteenth Article they receive the first part, in which we say that such ecclesiastical rites are to be observed as can be observed without sin and are of profit in the Church for tranquility and good order. They altogether condemn the second part, in which we say that human traditions instituted to appease God, to merit grace, and make satisfactions for sins are contrary to the Gospel. Although in the *Confession* itself, when treating of the distinction of meats, we have spoken at sufficient length concerning traditions, yet certain things should be briefly recounted here. *[Key to the Wittenberg reformers' view of church traditions is that they are often "works" that people do to earn God's grace. If grace cannot be earned, many traditions are unnecessary.]*

Although we supposed that the adversaries would defend human traditions on other grounds, yet we did not think that this would come to pass, namely, that they would condemn this article: that we do not merit the remission of sins or grace by the observance of human traditions. Since, therefore, this article has been condemned, we have an easy and plain case. The adversaries are now openly Judaizing, are openly suppressing the Gospel by the doctrines of demons. For Scripture calls traditions doctrines of demons, when it is taught that religious rites are serviceable to merit the remission of sins and grace. For they are then obscuring the Gospel, the benefit of Christ and the righteousness of faith. For they are just as directly contrary to Christ and to the Gospel as are fire and water to one another. The Gospel teaches that by faith we receive freely, for Christ's sake, the remission of sins and are reconciled to God. The adversaries, on the other hand, appoint another mediator, namely, these traditions. On account of these they wish to acquire remission of sins; on account of these they wish to appease God's wrath. But Christ clearly says, Matt. 15:9: "In vain do they worship me, teaching for doctrines the commandments of men."

But we cheerfully maintain the old traditions (as, the three high festivals, the observance of Sunday, and the like) made in the Church for the sake of usefulness and tranquility; and we interpret them in a more moderate way, to the exclusion of the opinion which holds that they justify.

And of the mortification of the flesh and discipline of the body we thus teach, just as the *Confession* states, that a true and not a feigned mortification occurs through the cross and afflictions by which God exercises us (when God breaks our will, inflicts the cross and trouble). In these we must obey God's will, as Paul says, Rom. 12:1: "Present your bodies a living sacrifice." . . . And this prescribed form of certain meats and times does nothing, as experience shows, towards curbing the flesh. For it is more luxurious and sumptuous than other feasts, for they were at greater expense, and practiced greater gluttony with fish and various Lenten meats than when the fasts were not observed, and not even the adversaries observe the form given in the canons.

Article XXII. Of Both Kinds in the Lord's Supper

It cannot be doubted that it is godly and in accordance with the institution of Christ and the words of Paul to use both parts in the Lord's Supper. For Christ instituted both parts and instituted them not for a part of the Church, but for the entire Church. For not only the priests, but the entire Church uses the Sacrament by the authority of Christ, and not by human authority; and this, we suppose, the adversaries acknowledge. Now, if Christ has instituted it for the entire Church, why is one kind denied to a part of the Church? Why is the use of the other kind prohibited? Why is the ordinance of Christ changed, especially when He Himself calls it His testament? But if it is not allowable to annul man's testament, much less will it be allowable to annul the testament of Christ. And Paul says, 1 Cor. 11:23, that he had received of the Lord that which he delivered. But he had delivered the use of both kinds, as the text, 1 Cor. 11, clearly shows. "This do in remembrance of Me," he says first concerning His body; afterwards he repeats the same words concerning the cup (the blood of Christ). And then: "Let a man examine himself, and so let him eat of that bread and drink of that cup." Here he names both. These are the words of Him who has instituted the Sacrament. And, indeed, he says before that those who will use the Lord's Supper should use both. It is evident, therefore, that the Sacrament was instituted for the entire Church. And the custom still remains in the Greek churches, and also once obtained in the Latin churches, as Cyprian and Jerome testify. *[Recall that "both kinds" refers to both the bread and the wine of the Last Supper.]*

The adversaries in the *Confutatio* do not endeavor to excuse the Church, to which one part of the Sacrament has been denied. This would have been becoming to good and religious men. For a strong reason for excusing the Church and instructing consciences to whom only a part of the Sacrament could be granted, should have been sought. Now these very men maintain that it is right to prohibit the other part and forbid that the use of both parts be allowed. First, they imagine that, in the beginning of the Church, it was the custom at some places that only one part was administered. Nevertheless, they are not able to produce any ancient example of this matter.

The Sacrament was instituted to console and comfort terrified minds, when they believe that the flesh of Christ, given for the life of the world, is food, when they believe that, being joined to Christ *[through this food]*, they are made alive. But the adversaries argue that laymen are removed from the other part as a punishment. "They ought," they say, "to be content." This is sufficient for a despot. But my lords, may we ask the reason, why ought they? "The reason must not be asked, but let whatever the theologians say be law." Is whatever you wish and whatever you say to be sheer truth? See now and be astonished how shameless and impudent the adversaries are: they dare to set up their own words as sheer commands of lords; they frankly say: The laymen must be content. But what if they must not? This is a concoction of Eck. For we recognize those vainglorious words, which if we would wish to criticize, there would be no want of language. For you see how great the impudence is.

They also allege the danger of spilling and certain similar things, which do not have force sufficient to change the ordinance of Christ. And, indeed, if we assume that we are free to use either one part or both, how can the prohibition to use both kinds be defended? Although the Church does not assume to itself the liberty to convert the ordinances of Christ into matters of indifference. We indeed excuse the Church which has borne the injury (the poor consciences which have been deprived of one part by force), since it could not obtain both parts; but the authors who maintain that the use of the entire Sacrament is justly prohibited, and who now not only prohibit, but even excommunicate and violently persecute those using an entire Sacrament, we do not excuse. Let them see to it how they will give an account to God for their decisions. Neither is it to be judged immediately that the Church determines or approves whatever the pontiffs determine, especially since Scripture prophesies concerning the bishops and pastors to effect this as Ezekiel 7:26 says: "The Law shall perish from the priest" (there will be priests or bishops who will know no command or law of God).

Article XXIII. Of the Marriage of Priests

Despite the great infamy of their defiled celibacy, the adversaries have the presumption not only to defend the pontifical law by the wicked and false pretext of the divine name, but even to exhort the Emperor and princes, to the disgrace and infamy of the Roman Empire, not to tolerate the marriage of priests. For thus they speak. Although the great, unheard-of lewdness, fornication, and adultery among priests, monks, etc., at the great abbeys, in other churches and cloisters, has become so notorious throughout the world that people sing and talk about it, still the adversaries who have presented the *Confutatio* are so blind and without shame that they defend the law of the Pope by which marriage is prohibited, and that, with the specious claim that they are defending a spiritual state. Moreover, although it would be proper for them to be heartily ashamed of the exceedingly shameful, lewd, abandoned, loose life of the wretches in their abbeys and cloisters, although on this account alone they should not have the courage to show their face in broad daylight, although their evil, restless heart and conscience ought to cause them to tremble, to stand aghast, and to be afraid to lift their eyes to our excellent Emperor, who loves uprightness.

And nevertheless they do not seriously defend celibacy. For they are not ignorant how few there are who practice chastity, but they stick to that comforting saying which is found in their treatise, *Si non caste, tamen caute* (If not chastely, at least cautiously), and they devise a sham of religion for their dominion, which they think that celibacy profits. They support their case with nothing but impious, hypocritical lies; accordingly, it will endure about as well as butter exposed to the sun. We cannot approve this law concerning celibacy which the adversaries defend, because it conflicts with divine and natural law, and is at variance with the very canons of the Councils. And that it is superstitious and dangerous is evident. For it produces infinite scandals, sins, and corruption of public morals.

Firstly, Genesis 1:28 teaches that men were created to be fruitful, and that one sex in a proper way should desire the other. For we are speaking not of concupiscence, which is sin, but of that appetite which was to have been in nature in its integrity which would have existed in nature even if it had remained uncorrupted, which they call physical love. And this love of one sex for the other is truly a divine ordinance. But since this ordinance of God cannot be removed without an extraordinary work of God, it follows that the right to contract marriage cannot be removed by statutes or vows. *["Concupiscence" is strong sexual desire or physical passion. Here, Melanchthon is drawing a distinction between love (good and natural) and lust (bad and sinful).]*

Secondly, And because this creation or divine ordinance in man is a natural right, jurists have accordingly said wisely and correctly that the union of male and female belongs to natural right. But since natural right is immutable, the right to contract marriage must always remain. For where nature does not change, that ordinance also with which God has endowed nature does not change, and cannot be removed by human laws.

Thirdly, Paul says, 1 Cor. 7:2: "To avoid fornication, let every man have his own wife." This now is an express command pertaining to all who are not fit for celibacy. The adversaries ask that a commandment be shown them which commands priests to marry. As though priests are not men! We judge indeed that the things which we maintain concerning human nature in general pertain also to priests. Does not Paul here command those who have not the gift of continence to marry? For he interprets himself a little after when he says, 7:9: "It is better to marry than to burn." Therefore all who burn, retain the right to marry. By this commandment of Paul: "To avoid fornication, let every man have his own wife," all are held bound who do not truly keep themselves continent; the decision concerning which pertains to the conscience of each one.

Fourthly, The pontifical law differs also from the canons of the Councils. For the ancient canons do not prohibit marriage, neither do they dissolve marriages that have been contracted. But the new canons, which have not been framed in the Synods, but have been made according to the private judgment of the Popes, both prohibit the contraction of marriages, and dissolve them when contracted; and this is to be done openly, contrary to the command of Christ, Matt. 19:6: "What God hath joined together, let not man put asunder." Therefore this law concerning perpetual celibacy is peculiar to this new pontifical despotism. Nor is it without a reason. For Daniel 11:37 ascribes to the kingdom of Antichrist this mark, namely, the contempt of women.

Fifthly, They proclaim that they require celibacy because it is purity. As though marriage were impurity and a sin, or as though celibacy merited justification more than does marriage! And to this end they cite the ceremonies of the Mosaic Law, because, since, under the Law, the priests, at the time of ministering, were separated from their wives, the priest in the New Testament, inasmuch as he ought always to pray, ought always to practice continence. This silly comparison is presented as a proof which should compel priests to perpetual celibacy. If purity is properly opposed to concupiscence, it signifies purity of heart, i.e., mortified concupiscence, because the Law does not prohibit marriage, but concupiscence, adultery, fornication. Therefore celibacy is not purity. For there may be greater purity of heart in a married man, as in Abraham or Jacob, than in most of those who are even truly continent (who even, according to bodily purity, really maintain their chastity).

Lastly, if they understand that celibacy is purity in the sense that it merits justification more than does marriage, we most emphatically contradict it. For we are justified neither on account of virginity nor on account of marriage, but freely for Christ's sake, when we believe that for His sake God is propitious to us. Neither does Christ or Paul praise virginity because it justifies, but because it is freer and less distracted with domestic occupations, in praying, teaching, writing, serving. For this reason Paul says, 1 Cor. 7:32: "He that is unmarried careth for the things which belong to the Lord." Virginity, therefore, is praised on account of meditation and study. Thus Christ does not simply praise those who make themselves eunuchs, but adds, for the kingdom of heaven's sake, i.e., that they may have leisure to learn or teach the Gospel; for He does not say that virginity merits the remission of sins or salvation.

Interrogations of Suspected Anabaptists (1528, 1533)

Augsburg's reluctance to take a firm position on religious practices, together with the frequent movement of people in and out of the city, meant that Anabaptists were prevalent in Augsburg. City authorities arrested and interrogated any Anabaptists they discovered. Luckily, interrogation records from sixteenth-century Augsburg have survived, so we can hear about the experiences of ordinary Anabaptists in their own words.

Source: Stadtarchiv Augsburg, Reichstadt Akten, Urgicht Agnes Vogel, 1528; Urgicht Barbara Nässlin, 1533; Urgicht Georg Nässlin, 1533; Urgicht Ursula Germair, 1533, all translated by B. Ann Tlusty. Agnes Vogel's interrogation is also excerpted in B. Ann Tlusty, ed., *Augsburg during the Reformation Era* (Indianapolis: Hackett, 2012).

Interrogation of Agnes Vogel

Agnes, the wife of soldier Paul Vogel, from Augsburg, says under questioning without torture:

She was rebaptized before the Feast of St. Michael (September 29) by the tailor Hans Leopold, in the upstairs room of a public house in Wellenburg. Also baptized at that time was a village boy that she doesn't know. She was moved to this baptism by the preachers here, for she went to their sermons for a good four years, while one preached this and the other that. One saw a symbol in the sacrament and the other would have it be flesh and blood. Thus they preached against one another, and made her all confused, so that she didn't know what to believe, and so she wanted to hear the others as well. For this reason she went out to Wellenburg with the shoemaker Simbrecht Widenman's wife and Rispin Pötin, and listened to the aforenoted Leopold's sermon. Based on what he taught her and what he showed her in the scriptures, she believed that if she followed him, she would be saved, and as noted above, she let herself be baptized. Before that she was never at a meeting, and also never knew or heard of any leader, and she also didn't know if Leopold was a leader or not.

After the baptism, she didn't go to any meetings except once when she was at the above noted Widenman's, and someone she didn't know was reading aloud there. There were around six or seven people there, and they said it wasn't a violation if so few people gathered, for the council had not forbidden that. Otherwise she would have stayed away from it.

After that the man who was reading aloud at Widenman's came to her house at around one o'clock in the afternoon, and stayed until about four o'clock. About six other people also came to her house. . . . Otherwise she didn't go anywhere where anyone was reading or teaching. She didn't give anyone anything or lodge anyone, and she can say nothing at all about their dealings or business.

Her husband doesn't know anything about her being rebaptized, and was not happy that their landlady, Mrs. Hafner, came to see her. And if her husband had found the leader in the house he would have thrown him down the stairs.

She doesn't know the person who read aloud, as she noted before. She also assumed he was a local person, since he was walking around openly in the streets. She didn't think that she was doing anything wrong by this or behaving in violation of an honorable council's rules.

Interrogation of Barbara and Georg Nässlin for Letting Anabaptists Meet in Their House
BARBARA NÄSSLIN

On March 5, 1533, Barbara, wife of Georg Nässlin, shoemaker of Augsburg, testified without torture:

It will be four years next Thursday since she was rebaptized. It was done by a superintendent named Philip in a house at Wertach Bridge where Stephan Mair, a weaver, lived, next to Geisselmaier's house where Erasmus Rieder now resides. She doesn't know if Philip is still alive or not.

Sebold the goldsmith and Georg the painter were at her house.

She didn't want to say any more, but when interrogated with thumb screws, she testified that also at her house were Philip, a locksmith at the city smithy; Kilian, an armor polisher on Burger Lane; Sabina Kretzwascher, the tailor's sister; a weaver called Hans from Ulm who is no longer in town; Ursula, her seamstress, she doesn't know where she is now working; Nesslerin's son Georg; plus a peasant called The Smith, she doesn't know where he is from; a boy from Ulm who has a master near Klenker Gate; Hans, a journeyman potmaker at Oschter's son-in-law; Hans in the blue hat; also a tailor with a beard whose shop is under the Mozarts' on the moat in front of Mendicant Gate; plus Hans Kard, weaver; and Berle, the wool finisher. They were also in her house.

The people named above all did readings, and he who received God's grace spoke.

She cannot and knows not how to give up the matter. She would rather leave her husband, who is not a part of it.

Sebald baptized Georg the painter in her house, and also an apprentice mason. He left for Neuburg about a year ago.

The brothers were not at her house more than three times at night. Otherwise they came and went daily by themselves, and two, three, four, or five at a time.

Captain Schludi also came and went at it pleased him, as he is free of duty. He would come and listen, then always left right away, and never joined in, but behaved as a man with nothing to do.

They were at Sabina Kreczwäscherin's twice, altogether about seven people, and they discussed God's word together.

Last summer she and her husband were at Seven Fountains Village where the above-named people also spoke together of God's word.

She knows nothing about going to temple or what it's about.

The largest meal that they had in her house was not over five pennies' worth.

When brothers arrived from out of town they came to her house with others named above, but not more than twice, once they bought shoes and once they didn't, and afterwards they left.

She knows of no other places where gatherings were held other than what is above.

She also knows of no other people associated with this that she can report. When her husband reproached her about it and tried to keep her from it, she told him that she would leave their household and follow them.

Her servant Leonhard was also an Anabaptist. He is pious and knows nothing but work. She doesn't know if he was put out of the city or not.

If she wanted to go out, she only had to do it secretly, but otherwise she didn't go anywhere other than as described above.

GEORG NÄSSLIN

Georg Nässlin, shoemaker from Augsburg, says under questioning without torture that he is not at all involved in the matter, except that when he didn't want to tolerate the brethren in his house, his wife said that she could not, would not, and did not wish to leave it alone—but if it had to be, she would as soon leave her husband. Upon that he decided, he is a craftsman who depends on some alms, which might be taken from him if he were hostile to the woman. And as it would be better to let them into his house than to bear and abide that his wife leave to go elsewhere, he tolerated the coming and going of the brethren in his house. . . . He has never been to a meeting and doesn't know of any other meetings. . . . His servant Leonhard, who has served him since Three Kings' Day, is also a brother. He was also here before and was escorted out of the city because he didn't want to take an oath at the Imperial Diet.

He doesn't know of any other activities that the brethren engaged in other than reading and talking.

Also asks of the Honorable Council that they decree that his wife be counseled away from this affair, whether by ministers or in another way.

Interrogation of Ursula Germair

Ursula Germair says under questioning without torture that she was baptized after last St. Jacob's Day (July 25). Sebold baptized her in Kreczwäscherin's house in the presence of Georg Maler and Kreczwäscherin. She has never been to any large meeting and knows of none. There were never more than four or five people there.

She only became involved in the matter after St. Jacob's Day. What happened before that she doesn't know. Sebold, Maler, [Sabina] Kreczwäscherin, [Barbara] Nässlin (as near as she can remember only once), a loden weaver named Sixt . . . , she said she never saw the watchmaker's wife, and two peasant women she didn't know gathered at the Kreczwäscherin's house. Once she was in the Nässlins' house with Georg Maler and Sebold. When they gathered, they talked of God's word.

She was never in a drinking bout. She didn't go there to drink wine but for heavenly sustenance. Aside from Kreczwäscherin's and Nässlin's house, she was not involved in it anywhere, and knows of no other place where they gather.

Even if My Lords, the Burgomaster and an Honorable Council were to let her out of jail and show her mercy, she still would not stay away from it, but would follow it to the end of her life.

She also saw the tailor who lives under the Mozarts go to Nässlin's house but had no other traffic with him.

She knows nothing about hanging up cloth or what it was about.

Acknowledgments

Norwich University students inspired the creation of this activity and brought it from prototype to finished product over many semesters of playtesting: they helped me perfect mechanics through their determination to "break" the game and their thoughtful reflections on the things they learned in the process. I also benefited from generous feedback shared by John Moser, Dwight Brautigam, Amy Curry, Tryntje Helfferich, and their students. At key points, B. Ann Tlusty and Amy Nelson Burnett identified sources and materials that let me expand and deepen engagement with complex historical realities.

The wonderful professional staff at the Stadtarchiv Augsburg and the Stadt- und Staatsbibliothek Augsburg cheerfully and efficiently found me the materials I needed to bring a fascinating set of historical circumstances to life. The faculty development program at Norwich University has consistently supported my work in German archives and libraries. And Austin, Lucy, and Gavin deserve credit for a lifetime of patience with my obsession with Augsburg, theology, and the social history of the Reformation.

Appendix
How to Find and Cite Passages from the Old or New Testament

The Christian Bible consists of two major sections, the Old Testament, which details God's revelations to the ancient Hebrew prophets, and the New Testament, which tells of events around and since the birth of Jesus Christ. The Gospels are the first four books of the New Testament and tell of events in the life of Jesus. The other books of the New Testament consist mainly of letters written by Peter, Paul, and other leaders of the early Christian church to congregations spread throughout the Mediterranean.

The earliest versions of the Bible were written in Greek, Latin, and Aramaic, and there are many different English translations. The translation directed by the king of England in 1611 and known as the King James Version (KJV) gives the scriptural English an old-fashioned poetic and weighty feel. But you may find that other translations, such as the New International Version (NIV) or New Revised Standard Version (NRSV), offer more clarity. Many websites offer the complete text of the Bible in various translations. Your instructor may suggest a specific translation to use during class.

CITING BIBLE PASSAGES

A Bible passage citation should include the following information: abbreviated book title (see standard abbreviations below), chapter number, and verse number(s). Chapter and verse are separated by a colon. For example, a citation to the fourteenth verse of the second chapter of Paul's first letter to the Corinthians would be written as 1 Cor. 2:14. The first ten verses of the second chapter of John would be written as John 2:1–10. Note that some older texts and translations may use slightly different conventions for citations or abbreviations.

STANDARD ABBREVIATIONS OF THE BOOKS OF THE NEW TESTAMENT

Acts of the Apostles	Acts
Colossians	Col.
1 Corinthians	1 Cor.
2 Corinthians	2 Cor.
Ephesians	Eph.
Galatians	Gal.
Hebrews	Heb.
James	James
John	John
1 John	1 John
2 John	2 John
3 John	3 John
Jude	Jude
Luke	Luke
Mark	Mark
Matthew	Matt.
1 Peter	1 Pet.
2 Peter	2 Pet.
Philemon	Philem.
Philippians	Phil.
Revelations	Rev.
Romans	Rom.
1 Thessalonians	1 Thess.
2 Thessalonians	2 Thess.
1 Timothy	1 Tim.
2 Timothy	2 Tim.
Titus	Titus

Glossary

absolution. One of the seven sacraments of the medieval church. A priest grants absolution as a formal forgiveness of sins after the person has confessed and performed acts of penance.

Anabaptist. General name for radical religious groups that shared certain characteristics in common, especially the belief that baptism should be freely chosen by adults.

anointing. One of the seven sacraments of the medieval church, also known as "last rites," meant to prepare a person for their possible or probable impending death.

baptism. One of the seven sacraments of the medieval church, and one of two accepted by Luther and Zwingli. A priest sprinkles or immerses a person—usually an infant—in water to wash them clean of original sin and allow them to enter the holy space of the church.

Bucer, Martin. A reformer who helped write the *Tetrapolitan Confession*. He spent much of his life trying to reconcile differences between Wittenberg and Swiss reformers.

Cajetan. A cardinal sent by the pope to meet with Martin Luther in Augsburg in 1518, and a major defender of the pope against the reformers. Also known by his given name, Tommaso de Vio.

canons / canon law. The collective traditions of the Roman church that have accumulated and been written down over time. A canon is also a type of priest.

celibacy. The act of refraining from all sexual relations and from marriage.

clergy/cleric. Refers to men who have been ordained as priests, including monks, canons, and friars. Bishops, archbishops, cardinals, and the pope are also considered clerics or members of the clergy.

confession. A statement of belief, as in the *Augsburg Confession*. Also, a verbal acknowledgment to a priest of sins that have been committed, done so that a priest can assign penance and grant absolution (forgiveness of confessed sins).

confirmation. One of the seven sacraments of the medieval church in which a person who was baptized as an infant has their identity as a Christian substantiated and sealed by a priest.

diocese. An administrative territory of the Roman church headed by a bishop or archbishop.

ecclesiastical. Having to do with the church.

Eck, Johann Maier von. A priest and theologian who defended the pope and the traditional Roman church against Luther's arguments and was not afraid to debate Luther in person. Primary author of the *Confutatio Pontificia*.

electors. The seven imperial rulers (three archbishops and four princes) who had the right to choose a new Holy Roman emperor.

Erasmus, Desiderius. A Dutch priest and brilliant humanist scholar who argued that the church needed to reform itself. He always remained loyal to the pope and the Roman church while frequently criticizing Luther.

Eucharist. Also known as Mass or the Lord's Supper, this sacrament is connected to the final meal Jesus shared with his followers before his death. In modern usage, it is often called Communion.

fasting. Going without food, or a particular type of food (usually meat), for a period of time.

friar. A type of priest who followed the rules of a monastic order (such as Franciscan or Augustinian) and pledged to primarily work out among the people and live a life of poverty.

Frosch, Johann. Abbot of the Carmelite Monastery of St. Anna in Augsburg and one of Martin Luther's first and most stalwart followers.

grace. Blessings or benefits from God that are given to humans. Traditionalists believed a person could demonstrate through their actions that they were worthy of the grace they received; reformers believed grace was entirely unmerited.

guilds. Self-governing professional organizations. They determined who could work in a particular profession, set standards for products, and played various other social and religious roles for their members.

gulden. A monetary unit in early modern Europe—a "gold coin." Sometimes referred to as a florin or guilder.

heretic. A person who openly defies the authority and teachings of the church or who embraces and advocates biblical or theological errors.

Holy Spirit. The third member of the trinity, alongside God the Father and the Son Jesus Christ. The Holy Spirit is the godly expression through which divine inspiration and knowledge can be made known to people.

iconoclasm. The removal of objects and images from a church, sometimes suddenly and violently.

idolatry. The worship of objects or images, or giving priority to any person, thing, or idea instead of God.

indulgence. A document granting the recipient a remission of some penalties for their sins.

laity/laypeople. Refers to people who have not become priests or other clergy within the church. All nonpriests, from ordinary people to kings and princes, are considered part of the laity.

Lent. A period of forty days before Easter. Medieval church tradition required people to abstain from eating meat, eggs, and dairy products during this time. Bread and vegetables were allowed, and occasionally fish.

limbo. A transitional state between heaven and hell where the souls of unbaptized infants reside forever. Unlike purgatory, souls may never be released from limbo.

Lord's Supper. Also known as Mass, the Eucharist, or Communion, it is a sacramental reenactment of the final meal Jesus had with his followers before his death.

Luther, Martin. An Augustinian friar in Wittenberg who sparked the Reformation with his 1517 publication of the *95 Theses*.

Mass. Any event in which the Eucharist is transubstantiated—whether or not people are present to witness.

Melanchthon, Philip. A pastor and close colleague of Martin Luther in Wittenberg. He wrote most of the *Augsburg Confession* and wrote the *Apology of the Augsburg Confession*.

memorandum. Formal statement of the findings of an investigation.

monk. A type of priest who lived with others in a monastery according to the rules of a monastic order, such as Benedictine or Dominican.

New Testament. Scripture detailing the life of Jesus (in the first four books, or Gospels) and instructional letters from early church leaders to Christian congregations.

Old Testament. Also known as the Hebrew Bible, this scripture recounts God's relationship with the Hebrew people before the coming of Jesus Christ.

ordination. One of the seven sacraments of the medieval church used to designate a person a new member of the clergy.

original sin. The residual uncleanness that all humans are born with due to the disobedience of humanity's first parents, Adam and Eve, in the Garden of Eden. Traditionalists believe that infant baptism is essential to remove original sin.

parish. The basic organizational unit of the Christian church—a small administrative district overseen by a member of the clergy.

patricians. Members of a small number of important, ancient families that established themselves as social, political, and economic leaders in the community.

penance. Prayers or other actions performed by a Christian to demonstrate that they are truly sorry for committing sin. Once penance is completed, a priest can grant absolution.

pope. The leader of the traditional Christian church in Rome, claiming authority that goes back to the Apostle Peter, appointed by Jesus to lead his followers after his death. The pope in 1530 was Clement VII.

purgatory. A state between heaven and hell where people could work off their remaining sins before being granted admission into heaven. Many reformers rejected a belief in purgatory.

Rhegius, Urbanus. The cathedral preacher in Augsburg who was an early follower of Martin Luther.

sacraments. Holy rituals performed by the clergy. Reformers recognized only two sacraments: the Eucharist and baptism. Traditionalists recognized five others: confirmation, marriage, ordination, absolution, and anointing (last rites).

saints. Exemplary Christians, both male and female, who experienced suffering due to their religious convictions and who have performed recognized miracles after their death.

salvation. The act of being "saved" from hell or purgatory and consequently admitted to heaven after death.

Schilling, Johann. A radical preacher in Augsburg whose departure led to a 1524 uprising against the city council.

Schmalkaldic League. An alliance of cities and territories aligned with the reforming principles of Wittenberg. It was organized in 1530 in the town of Schmalkalden by Philip of Hesse and Johann Friedrich of Saxony to protect territories that chose to reform.

Sturm, Jakob. A reformer in the city of Strasbourg and related to members of Augsburg's patrician Rehlinger family. Sturm supported a Swiss-style reform but had a close relationship with the Schmalkaldic League.

Swabian League. A military alliance of southern German cities and territories. Formed in 1488, it began to fall apart in the late 1520s due to disagreements about the Reformation.

Tetrapolitan. From the Latin, "four cities," this term was used to designate the Swiss reform-oriented cities who offered the emperor an alternate written confession in 1530: Memmingen, Lindau, Constance, and Strasbourg.

Three-Cities League. An alliance between Augsburg, Nuremberg, and Ulm.

transubstantiation. The process by which bread and wine become the literal body and blood of Jesus. The appearance stays the same, but the substance is transformed by the prayer of a priest.

wafer. A small, thin morsel of bread often shared during the Eucharist.

works. Anything people do in hopes of improving their chances of getting to heaven, including fasting, praying to saints, going on pilgrimage, and buying indulgences. Luther and Zwingli both argued that works did not impact salvation.

Zwingli, Ulrich. A reformer from Zurich, Switzerland, who developed a system of reform parallel to Martin Luther's. He was killed in battle in 1531.

Selected Bibliography of English-Language Sources

PRIMARY SOURCE ANTHOLOGIES

Bromiley, G. W., ed. *Zwingli and Bullinger: Selected Translations*. Library of Christian Classics, vol. 24. Sacramento: Hassell Street Press, 2021.

Graham, M. Patrick, ed. *Luther as Heretic: Ten Catholic Responses to Martin Luther, 1518–1541*. Cambridge, UK: James Clarke, 2020.

Mangrum, Bryan D., and Giuseppe Scavizzi, eds. *A Reformation Debate: Karlstadt, Emser, and Eck on Sacred Images*. Toronto: Centre for Reformation and Renaissance Studies, 1998.

Pipkin, H. Wayne, ed. *Selected Writings of Huldrych Zwingli*. Pittsburgh Theological Monographs. Allison Park, PA: Pickwick, 1984.

Porter, J. M., ed. *Luther: Selected Political Writings*. Eugene, OR: Wipf and Stock, 2003.

Tappert, Theodore G., ed. *Selected Writings of Martin Luther*. Minneapolis: Fortress, 2007.

Tlusty, B. Ann, ed. *Augsburg during the Reformation Era: An Anthology of Sources*. Indianapolis: Hackett, 2012.

SECONDARY SOURCES

The Early Reformation in Augsburg

Broadhead, Philip. "Guildsmen, Religious Reform and the Search for the Common Good: The Role of the Guilds in the Early Reformation in Augsburg." *Historical Journal* 39, no. 3 (1996): 577–97.

Creasman, Allyson. *Censorship and Civic Order in Reformation Germany, 1517–1648: "Printed Poison and Evil Talk."* Farnham, UK: Ashgate, 2012.

Hanson, Michele Zelinsky. *Religious Identity in an Early Reformation Community: Augsburg, 1517 to 1555*. Leiden: Brill, 2009.

Roper, Lyndal. *The Holy Household: Religion and Morals in Reformation Augsburg*. Oxford: Oxford University Press, 1989.

Tlusty, B. Ann, and Mark Häberlein, eds. *A Companion to Late Medieval and Early Modern Augsburg*. Leiden: Brill, 2020.

Van Amberg, Joel. *A Real Presence: Religious and Social Dynamics of the Eucharistic Conflicts in Early Modern Augsburg, 1520–1530*. Leiden: Brill, 2012.

Business and Economics in Augsburg

Häberlein, Mark. *The Fuggers of Augsburg: Pursuing Wealth and Honor in Renaissance Germany*. Charlottesville: University of Virginia Press, 2012.

Safley, Thomas Max. *The History of Bankruptcy: Economic, Social and Cultural Implications in Early Modern Europe*. Hoboken: Taylor and Francis, 2013.

Tlusty, B. Ann. "Full Cups, Full Coffers: Tax Strategies and Consumer Culture in the Early Modern German Cities." *German History* 32, no. 1 (2014): 1–28.

Reformation Politics in the Holy Roman Empire

Brady, Thomas A. *Protestant Politics: Jakob Sturm (1489–1553) and the German Reformation*. Atlantic Highlands, NJ: Humanities Press, 1995.

Close, Christopher. *The Negotiated Reformation: Imperial Cities and the Politics of Urban Reform, 1525–1550*. New York: Cambridge University Press, 2009.

Moeller, Bernd. *Imperial Cities and the Reformation*. Philadelphia: Fortress, 1972.

Whitford, David M. *A Reformation Life: The European Reformation through the Eyes of Philipp of Hesse*. Santa Barbara: Praeger, 2015.

Wilson, Peter H. *Heart of Europe: A History of the Holy Roman Empire*. Cambridge, MA: Belknap Press of Harvard University Press, 2016.

The Eucharistic Controversy

Burnett, Amy Nelson. *Debating the Sacraments: Print and Authority in the Early Reformation*. New York: Oxford University Press, 2019.

———. *Karlstadt and the Origins of the Eucharistic Controversy: A Study in the Circulation of Ideas*. New York: Oxford University Press, 2011.

Wandel, Lee Palmer, ed. *A Companion to the Eucharist in the Reformation*. Leiden: Brill, 2014.

———. *The Eucharist in the Reformation: Incarnation and Liturgy*. New York: Cambridge University Press, 2006.

The Reformation and Reformers

Eire, Carlos M. N. *Reformations: The Early Modern World, 1450–1650*. New Haven, CT: Yale University Press, 2016.

Gordon, Bruce. *The Swiss Reformation.* New Frontiers in History. Manchester: Manchester University Press, 2002.

———. *Zwingli: God's Armed Prophet.* New Haven, CT: Yale University Press, 2021.

Horton, Michael Scott. *Reformation Theology: A Systematic Summary.* Wheaton, IL: Crossway, 2017.

Massing, Michael. *Fatal Discord: Erasmus, Luther, and the Fight for the Western Mind.* New York: HarperCollins, 2018.

Pettegree, Andrew. *Brand Luther: 1517, Printing, and the Making of the Reformation.* New York: Penguin Books, 2016.

———. *Reformation and the Culture of Persuasion.* Cambridge: Cambridge University Press, 2005.

Roper, Lyndal. *Living I Was Your Plague: Martin Luther's World and Legacy.* Princeton, NJ: Princeton University Press, 2021.

———. *Martin Luther: Renegade and Prophet.* New York: Random House, 2018.

Rublack, Ulinka. *Reformation Europe.* Cambridge: Cambridge University Press, 2017.

www.ingramcontent.com/pod-product-compliance
Lightning Source LLC
Chambersburg PA
CBHW060319190925
32849CB00006B/96